THE OFFICIAL
TOTTENHAM HOTSPUR
QUIZ BOOK

COMPILED BY JOHN DT WHITE
Foreword by Gary Mabbutt MBE and Pat Jennings OBE

APEX PUBLISHING LTD

First published in 2005, Reprinted and Updated in 2006 & 2007 & 2008 by

Apex Publishing Ltd

PO Box 7086, Clacton on Sea, Essex, CO15 5WN, England

www.apexpublishing.co.uk

Copyright © 2005-2008 by John DT White
The author has asserted his moral rights

British Library Cataloguing-in-Publication Data
A catalogue record for this book
is available from the British Library

ISBN 1-904444-44-X   978-1-904444-44-2

Typeset in 10.5pt Clarity Gothic Light SF

Production Manager: Chris Cowlin

Printed in Great Britain by the MPG Books Group, Bodmin and King's Lynn

Cover Design: Andrew Macey
The club badge was kindly supplied by Tottenham Hotspur FC

This book is an official product of Tottenham Hotspur FC

Dedication:
This book is dedicated to my family and friends who mean everything to me. I wish to thank you all personally for your love, support and friendship.
Yours,
John

FOREWORD

We are delighted to write the Foreword for John's Official Tottenham Hotspur Quiz Book. We are also delighted that John and his publisher, Apex Publishing Limited, have very kindly agreed to donate £1 to the Willow Foundation from every copy of this book sold, especially as we are both patrons of this fabulous charity.

The Willow Foundation was founded by our great friend Bob Wilson and his wife, in 1999, when their daughter Anna died of cancer at the age of 31. It is a registered charity (www.willowfoundation.org.uk) dedicated to improving the quality of life of seriously ill young adults aged 16 to 40 throughout the UK, by organising and funding a 'Special Day' of their choice. Special Days give young people with life-threatening or life-limiting conditions a chance to escape the difficulties of their daily routine and share quality time with family and friends while pursuing an activity they can all enjoy. A Special Day could be a trip to a health farm or a visit to a pop concert; an afternoon of Premiership Football or a flight on the British Airways London Eye. The Willow Foundation's aim is to be able to arrange a Special Day of their choice for every seriously ill young adult in the UK. Your contribution from the purchase of this book will help fund such Special Days.

As we all know, Spurs is a club steeped in tradition and was founded in 1882 by boys from Hotspur Cricket Club; however, we won't go into any historical detail here as John has a section in the book covering this very subject. Enough to say that, as players of the past with nearly 1,200 appearances between us, we both enjoyed much success at the Club and always appreciated the support of some of the most loyal fans in the country.

This book is a trip through 125 years, from the Club's beginnings to the current 2006-2007 Premier League season. There are over 1,000 questions in the book that will test and tease you for hours and just about every subject you can think of has been covered including: our

Double season, FA Cup triumphs, League Cup triumphs, League Championship successes, managers, European triumphs, trivia, past legends and questions on the present-day side.

We can both thoroughly recommend this book to all Spurs fans and, by buying it, you are also helping someone less fortunate than yourself.

Yours forever Spurs,

Gary Mabbutt and Pat Jennings

INTRODUCTION

I was inspired to write this book by 2 men, Chris Cowlin at Apex Publishing Limited and a Spurs Legend who my Father and I share the same name with, John White.

In writing this book I would like to say a special word of thanks to a few people who all played an important role in helping me out. I would like to thank David Williams at The Willow Foundation in securing Gary & Pat to write the Foreword for my book. A number of sources were used to help me compile my questions including *www.mehstg.co.uk*. I would also like to thank David Buchler, Donna Cullen, John Fennelly, Fran Jones and Andy Porter at Tottenham Hotspur Football Club for all their hard work. And finally, I would like to say thanks to everyone who was kind enough to write a few lines in support of the book including Keith Burkinshaw, Cliff Jones, Martin Jol, Robbie Keane, Ledley King, John Motson and last but certainly not least, Jurgen Klinsmann.

Spurs motto "Audere Est Facere" means "To Dare Is To Do". This motto is very applicable to me personally because I have done many things in my life that many people told me that there was no point in me trying to do. However, I dared and on many occasions it paid off. Ask yourself when was the last time you dared to do something only to give up on your initial thought. So in closing, never give up on your dreams; never give in easily; never be negative about yourself and above all else, never say never.

And always remember, Audere Est Facere.

Best wishes
John DT White

www.apexpublishing.co.uk

BILL NICHOLSON

1. Where was Bill born - Scarborough, Scunthorpe or Southend?

2. In which year did he make his league debut for Spurs - 1936, 1937 or 1938?

3. In which position did Bill play in his early days for Spurs?

4. How many full international caps did Bill win for England?

5. What was unusual about Bill's first kick of the ball when he made his full international debut for England?

6. Name the famous university team, better known for rowing, that Bill coached.

7. Which team was Bill one of the coaches of in 1958 in Sweden?

8. Can you recall the year he was appointed manager of Spurs - 1958, 1959 or 1960?

9. In which season did Bill resign as Spurs manager?

10. Who succeeded Bill as manager of Spurs?

SEASON 2004 - 2005

11. Who did Spurs play on the opening day of the season?

12. Following on from Q11, what was the score of the game -
1-1, 2-2 or 3-3?

13. Against which team did Spurs record their first Premier League
win of the season?

14. Can you recall who was the Spurs goalscorer when they beat
Birmingham City 1-0 in August?

15. When Spurs drew 0-0 at Chelsea, what did the Chelsea
Manager claim Spurs brought onto the pitch with them?

16. Who did Spurs beat 6-0 away in the Carling Cup?

17. Name the first team that beat Spurs in the Premiership.

18. Can you recall the team to which Spurs lost 2-1 at home to and
then beat 4-3 away only 4 days later, during October?

19. With which London club did Spurs draw 1-1 at home with in
their last game of 2004?

20. Name the first team that Spurs beat in 2005.

ROBBIE KEANE

21. Robbie made his senior debut for the Republic of Ireland in Olomouc in March 1999. Name the country the Irish played.

22. At which club did Robbie begin his Professional career?

23. Name the "City" that Robbie signed for after he left the club in Q22.

24. Robbie only spent one season at the club in Q23. Can you name the Serie A club he then joined?

25. Following on from Q24, what English club did Robbie join after leaving this team?

26. In which year did he sign for Spurs?

27. Against which London club did he make his Spurs debut?

28. How many games into his Spurs career was it before Robbie scored?

29. What Lancashire club did Robbie support as a boy?

30. Whose Republic of Ireland international goal scoring record did Robbie Keane surpass when he scored his 22nd goal for his country?

THE DOUBLE

31.   In which season did Spurs do the "Double"?

32.   How many of their home games in the League did they win - 15, 16 or 17?

33.   Name the Lancashire team that Spurs beat 2-0 at White Hart Lane on the opening day of the season.

34.   How many League games did Spurs win in a row from the start of the season?

35.   Which team were the first to beat Spurs in the League - Arsenal, Manchester United or Sheffield Wednesday?

36.   At which Midland club's ground did Spurs play their FA Cup Semi-Final?

37.   Can you name the London club that Spurs beat in the FA Cup 3rd Round?

38.   To the nearest 25, how many goals did Spurs score in their 42 League games?

39.   Who did Spurs beat in the FA Cup Final?

40.   How many of their away games in the League did they win - 14, 15 or 16?

LEGEND -
DANNY BLANCHFLOWER

41.   Where was Danny born - Belfast, Lisburn or Londonderry?

42.   At which Irish League club did Danny begin his Professional career?

43.   Name the Yorkshire club he signed for after he left the club in Q42.

44.   Danny only spent 2 seasons at the club in Q43. Can you name the Midlands club he then joined?

45.   Name the home nation against which Danny made his full international debut for Northern Ireland.

46.   In which year's World Cup Finals did he represent Northern Ireland?

47.   Which other London club was involved in a bidding war with Spurs for Danny's services before he finally moved to White Hart Lane?

48.   To the nearest £5,000, how much did Danny cost Spurs?

49.   Which Cup did Danny win with Spurs in 1963?

50.   Which London club did Danny manage after he stepped down as manager of Northern Ireland?

LEGEND - GARY LINEKER

51.   Where in England was Gary born?

52.   At which League club did Gary begin his Professional career -
        Aston Villa, Glasgow Rangers or Leicester City?

53.   Name the English club that he signed for in 1985.

54.   Gary only spent 1 season at the club in Q53. Can you name the
        Primera Liga club he then joined?

55.   In which year did he make his full international debut for
        England - 1983, 1984 or 1985?

56.   Name the home nation which Gary made his full international
        debut against.

57.   To the nearest 5, how many goals did he score for England
        in full internationals?

58.   Which was the first trophy that Gary won at club level in his
        Professional career?

59.   Name the only trophy that Gary won with Spurs.

60.   Who was Gary's manager when he played for Grampus Eight
        in Japan?

KEITH BURKINSHAW

61. In which year did Keith take up his first coaching job at Spurs?

62. What was his first job at the club?

63. Name the Spurs manager when Keith arrived.

64. In which year was Keith appointed manager of Spurs?

65. Can you name the "Town" that were Spurs' first opponents with Keith as the Tottenham Hotspur manager?

66. Before arriving at White Hart Lane, was Keith the caretaker manager of Scarborough, Scunthorpe or Stockport County?

67. What happened to Spurs at the end of Keith's first season in charge?

68. What was the highest position in which Spurs finished in the First Division with Keith as their manager?

69. Name the first domestic trophy that Spurs won under Keith's management.

70. At the end of which season did Keith leave White Hart Lane?

UEFA CUP WINNERS 1984

71.   Name the manager who led Spurs to UEFA Cup success in 1984.

72.   Which team did Spurs beat in the Final?

73.   Can you recall the score of the 1st Leg of the Final that Spurs played away?

74.   Can you recall the score of the 2nd Leg of the Final at White Hart Lane?

75.   Following on from Q73 and Q74, name any Spurs goalscorer in the Final.

76.   Can you recall the Irish "United" that Spurs met in the 1st Round of the 1983-84 UEFA Cup?

77.   Who were Spurs' opponents in the Semi-Final?

78.   Name the German club that beat Spurs 1-0 in Germany but lost 2-0 to Spurs at White Hart Lane in the 3rd Round.

79.   Can you name the Austrian team that Spurs met in the competition?

80.   Which one of Spurs' opponents did they beat on the away goals rule in the competition?

HISTORY

81.   In which year was the club formed?

82.   What was the first name the club was known by?

83.   The club was formed by members of a local club. What sport
        did the members of the local club play?

84.   Can you recall the name of the team that the club played for
        the first of many times on 19 November 1887?

85.   What colour of shirts or shorts were adopted by the club in
        1890?

86.   Against what "County" did Spurs play their first match at their
        new home, White Hart Lane?

87.   What did Spurs achieve in 1901 that no other club has ever
        repeated?

88.   Spurs played their first Football League match in 1908. Which
        "Wanderers" provided the opposition?

89.   What did Spurs win in 1920?

90.   The Spurs motto is "Audere est Facere" but what does it mean?

IT HAPPENED THIS YEAR

*ALL YOU HAVE TO DO HERE IS ASSOCIATE THE EVENT
WITH THE YEAR IT HAPPENED*

91.	Spurs appear in their 8th FA Cup Final	1961
92.	Kit is changed to white shirts and shorts	1988
93.	UEFA Cup winners	1985
94.	Spurs sign their first "£1 million plus" player	1982
95.	Club Shield introduced	1973
96.	New West Stand opened	1938
97.	Promotion to Division 1	1957
98.	Spurs first played in European competition	1987
99.	League Cup winners	1978
100.	Record attendance for White Hart Lane set	1972

WINNERS

*ALL YOU HAVE TO DO HERE IS ASSOCIATE THE
COMPETITION WITH THE YEAR SPURS WON IT*

101.	Anglo-Italian League Cup	1950
102.	European Cup Winners' Cup	1910
103.	Football League Cup	1900
104.	Football League Division 1	1971
105.	Football League Division 2	1921
106.	FA Charity Shield (Joint Winners)	1902
107.	Dewar Shield	1999
108.	FA Cup	1963
109.	London Challenge Cup	1967
110.	Southern League	1951

TRIVIA - 1

111.   Can you name Spurs' first "£1 million plus" signing?

112.   What were Spurs the first football club to do in 1983?

113.   Which part of White Hart Lane became an all-seater enclosure in 1994?

114.   Who in 1995 became Spurs' new record signing?

115.   Who was the manager of Spurs when they were relegated to Division 2 in 1977?

116.   Name any year in which Gary Lineker was voted the Football Writers' Association Footballer of the Year.

117.   Which was the first major cup competition won by the club?

118.   Who in 1981 set a new club record of League appearances?

119.   Following on from Q118, whose previous record did he beat?

120.   Can you name the FA Cup winners of 1983 that Spurs beat in the 1983 Sun International Challenge Trophy in Swaziland?

DIMITAR BERBATOV

121.   In which year did Dimitar sign for Spurs?

122.   From which Bundesliga club did Spurs sign Dimitar?

123.   How much did Spurs pay for the services of Dimitar - £10.9m, £11.9m or £12.9m?

124.   Name the team Dimitar scored 4 goals against on 29th December 2007.

125.   Can you recall the team where Dimitar began his professional career in his home country?

126.   Which Premiership club was Dimitar strongly linked with a move to in January 2008?

127.   In which year was Dimitar first capped at full international level by Bulgaria?

128.   To the nearest 5 how many international goals had Dimitar scored at 1st January 2008?

129.   Against which Lancashire club did Dimitar make his Premier League debut for Spurs, a 2-0 away defeat?

130.   Name the "United" Dimitar scored his first Premiership goal for Spurs against.

THE MANAGERS

ALL YOU HAVE TO DO HERE IS ASSOCIATE THE MANAGER WITH HIS PERIOD IN CHARGE

131.	Peter Shreeves	2001-2003
132.	Ossie Ardiles	1986-1987
133.	George Graham	1991-1992
134.	David Pleat	1994-1997
135.	Keith Burkinshaw	1997-1998
136.	Peter Shreeves	1987-1991
137.	Terry Venables	1993-1994
138.	Gerry Francis	1998-2001
139.	Christian Gross	1984-1986
140.	Glenn Hoddle	1976-1984

LEGEND - JURGEN KLINSMANN

141.　In which year did Jurgen join Spurs for the first time?

142.　Following on from Q141, from what club did Spurs sign Jurgen?

143.　Can you name either of the 2 Romanian players that also joined Spurs at the same time when Jurgen first signed?

144.　Name the Spurs manager who brought Jurgen to White Hart Lane in Q141.

145.　Following on from Q141, how many seasons did he stay at Spurs during his first period at the club?

146.　Name the club that Jurgen joined when he first left Spurs.

147.　What did he win in his first season with the team he joined in Q146?

148.　Jurgen won a UEFA Cup winners medal in 1991. Which Serie A side did he play for at the time?

149.　Name the Italian club he signed for in 1997.

150.　In which year did he win the World Cup with Germany?

HAT-TRICKS

*ALL YOU HAVE TO DO HERE IS ASSOCIATE THE PLAYER
WITH THE TEAM HE SCORED A HAT-TRICK AGAINST*

151.	Jurgen Klinsmann	Derby County - 8 September 1990
152.	Jermain Defoe	Coventry City - 28 March 1992
153.	Gordon Durie	Bolton - 11 December 2001
154.	Frederic Kanoute	Southampton - 11 March 2000
155.	Robbie Keane	Wimbledon - 2 May 1998
156.	Teddy Sheringham	QPR - 30 September 1989
157.	Gary Lineker	Crystal Palace - 3 January 2004
158.	Les Ferdinand	Hereford United - 17 January 1996
159.	Paul Gascoigne	Southampton - 18 December 2004
160.	Steffen Iversen	Everton - 12 January 2003

SEASON 2003-2004

161. What Midlands club did Spurs lose 1-0 to on the opening day of the season?

162. How many Premier League games did Spurs win - 13, 14 or 15?

163. Can you name the London club who Spurs beat in the 3rd Round of the FA Cup?

164. Spurs' first win in the League was a 2-1 victory over Leeds United at White Hart Lane on 23 August. Name either of the 2 Spurs goalscorers.

165. Which "City" did Spurs beat in Round 2 of the League Cup?

166. Who scored against one of his former clubs on the last day of the season?

167. Name either of the 2 South African teams which Spurs played against in a pre-season friendly before the 2003-2004 commenced.

168. Can you name the Spurs player who, on 29 October 2003 in a League Cup 3rd Round tie, scored against the team he would eventually leave Spurs to join?

169. The eventual winners of the League Cup put Spurs out of the competition in Round 5. Name them.

170. Which team were Spurs leading 3-0 in an FA Cup 4th Round Replay at White Hart Lane only to lose the game 4-3?

TRMA - 2

171. In which year did Gary Lineker win the PFA Player of the Year Award - 1985, 1986 or 1987?

172. Which former Spurs player was nicknamed "The Golden Bomber"?

173. Name the Spurs manager who signed Steve Archibald.

174. What is Spurs' highest ever finish in the Premier League?

175. Following on from Q174, in what season did they achieve this?

176. Name the Spurs striker who scored a hat-trick against a former club of his in a Premier League game at White Hart Lane on 6 December 2003.

177. Can you name the Belgian team that Spurs beat in the Final of the Costa Del Sol Tournament in 1965?

178. Who in 1997 became Spurs' new record signing?

179. Can you name the striker who joined Spurs from a Serie A club in January 1998?

180. What was Spurs' final placing in the 2003-04 Premier League season - 12th, 13th or 14th?

LEGEND - CLIFF JONES

181.   In which year did Cliff join Spurs - 1957, 1958 or 1959?

182.   Apart from football, name either of the 2 principal sports that Cliff played when he served in the Army prior to arriving at White Hart Lane.

183.   From which Welsh club did Jimmy Anderson sign Cliff for Spurs?

184.   In which position did Cliff play for Spurs?

185.   How old was Cliff when he won his first full international cap for Wales?

186.   What was Cliff the first of for Spurs in the 1967 FA Cup Final against Chelsea?

187.   In which year did Cliff leave White Hart Lane - 1967, 1968 or 1969?

188.   Can you recall the London team he joined after leaving Spurs?

189.   What injury did Cliff sustain soon after returning from the 1958 World Cup Finals?

190.   To the nearest 25, how many career goals did Cliff score for Spurs in all matches, including friendlies?

SEASON 2005-2006

191. Can you name the Spurs player who was the first to score for the club in the FA Premier League during the season?

192. Spurs beat the 2003 UEFA Cup winners 2-0 in a pre-season friendly at White Hart Lane. Name the team.

193. This City put Spurs out of the FA Cup in Round 3. Name them.

194. Name the London club that inflicted Spurs' first league defeat on them during the season.

195. This defender earned Spurs a point against Arsenal at White Hart Lane. Name him.

196. Can you name the Town that knocked Spurs out of the League Cup in Round 2?

197. Spurs beat Olympique Lyonnais 3-1 in a Cup Final on 24th July 2005. What Cup did they win?

198. Three Spurs players scored a penalty for the club in a league game during the season. Name any 2 of the 3.

199. Who scored his last league goal for Spurs in their 2-1 home win over Manchester City on 8th April 2006?

200. Can you name the team Spurs lost 2-1 away at on the last day of the season?

SEASON 2006-07 - 1

201.   In which position did Spurs finish in the Premiership?

202.   Against which Yorkshire club did Spurs record their first Premiership win of the season?

203.   How many of their 38 Premiership games did Spurs win?

204.   Spurs beat this Midlands club 2-1 at White Hart Lane on Boxing Day. Name them.

205.   Can you recall the club Paul Robinson scored agaisnt on St Patrick's Day 2007 in a 2-1 win for Spurs at White Hart Lane?

20.6.   Spurs drew 1-1 away to this club on New Year's Day 2007. Can you name them?

207.   This Italian side lost 2-1 to Spurs in a pre-season friendly at White Hart Lane on 30th July 2006 but went on to win Serie A in season 2006-07. Name them.

208.   Name the "City" Spurs beat 4-0 at White Hart Lane in an FA Cup 3rd Round Replay.

209.   To the nearest 5 how many Premier League points did Spurs end the season with?

210.   This Spurs defender scored his first goal for the club in the 1-1 Premiership draw away to Fulham on 20 January 2007. Name him.

LEGEND - PAUL GASCOIGNE - 1

211.   At which club did Paul start his Professional career?

212.   How many seasons did he spend in the first team at the club in Q211?

213.   To the nearest 10, how many competitive appearances did he make for Spurs?

214.   In which year did Gazza sign for Spurs?

215.   Which club did he join after leaving White Hart Lane?

216.   Can you recall the Spurs manager who signed Gazza?

217.   At which World Cup Finals did Gazza cry?

218.   Name the club he signed for after leaving the team in Q215.

219.   Apart from Spurs and the team in Q211, name any other English Premier League side he played for.

220.   Name the Lancashire team he joined in 2002.

LEDLEY KING

221.   In which season did Ledley make his FA Premier League debut for Spurs?

222.   Can you recall the Lancashire club against which Ledley made his FA Premier League debut for Spurs?

223.   What age was Ledley when he made his league debut for Spurs?

224.   Ledley has 3 nicknames at the club. Can you name any 2 of them?

225.   Which squad number did Ledley wear for Spurs during 2006/2007?

226.   Can you recall the year Ledley signed trainee forms with Spurs?

227.   Which goal scoring FA Premier League record does Ledley currently hold?

228.   In which year did Ledley win his first senior international cap for England?

229.   Can you name the England manager who awarded Ledley his first senior international cap for his country?

230.   What national descent are Ledley's parents?

TRMA - 3

231.   In which year did Jurgen Klinsmann captain Germany to European Championship success?

232.   Which "City" did Spurs meet in both the FA Cup and League Cup during season 2003-2004?

233.   When did Martin Jol win as his first Barclays Premier League Manager of the Month award?

234.   What is Spurs' lowest ever finish in the Premier League?

235.   Following on from Q234, in which season did they finish in this position?

236.   Can you name the man that managed Paul Gascoigne at both club and full international level?

237.   Against which North East club did Spurs record their biggest Premier League win during the 2002-2003 season?

238.   How many full international appearances did Gary Lineker make for England - 80, 90 or 100?

239.   What was Spurs' last game under the management of Keith Burkinshaw?

240.   Name the Scottish "United" that Spurs beat to win the Japan Cup in 1979.

SPURS v ARSENAL - 1

241.   Up to the end of 2004, who was the last senior Spurs player to leave White Hart Lane and join Arsenal?

242.   Can you name the "Chris" who made his debut for Spurs against Arsenal on 13 October 1973?

243.   Which "Pat" played his last League game for Spurs against Arsenal on 11 May 1993?

244.   Following on from Q243, name the Spurs hardman that also made his last appearance for the club in the same game.

245.   This "John" made his debut for Spurs against Arsenal in March 1969 and later the same year scored his first goal for Spurs in a game against Arsenal. Name him.

246.   Can you name the player who scored his first goal for Spurs in a game against Arsenal at White Hart Lane on 13 November 2004?

247.   This Romanian international scored his last goal for Spurs in a match against Arsenal on 2 January 1995. Name him.

248.   What was significant about the Spurs v Arsenal match played on 8 April 2001?

249.   Name the Spurs player who made his 500th senior appearance for the club against Arsenal on 27 September 1975.

250.   Who made the 150th League appearance of his career in the match against Arsenal on 13 November 2004?

SPURS v CHELSEA

251. Up to the end of 2004, who was the last player to join Chelsea from Spurs?

252. Name the former Spurs hero who scored twice for Chelsea against Spurs in their 3-1 win in September 1986?

253. This Scottish striker joined Spurs from Chelsea for £2 million in August 1991. Name him.

254. Can you name the former Spurs Reserve Team player who scored for Chelsea against Spurs in a 1-1 draw in November 1984?

255. In managerial terms, what was significant about the Spurs v Chelsea game in Q254?

256. Name the former Rangers player who scored for Spurs in a win against Chelsea on 19 April 1975.

257. Following on from Q256, name the famous World Cup referee with who officiated the game.

258. Name the Scottish teenager who made his Spurs debut as a substitute against Chelsea on 3 April 1974.

259. Which "Steve" was reputedly the first Premier League player to pull his shirt over his head in celebrating a goal for Spurs against Chelsea on 27 February 1994?

260. Up to the end of 2004, who was the last player to join Spurs from Chelsea?

LEGEND - STEVE PERRYMAN

261.   At which London club did Steve begin his career as an
        Apprentice footballer?

262.   In which year did Steve make his debut for Spurs?

263.   What was the first trophy that Steve won as a first team player
        at Spurs?

264.   In which year did Steve win his first FA Cup winners' medal?

265.   What age was Steve when he won his first full international cap
        for England - 28, 29 or 30?

266.   Can you recall the award Steve won in 1982?

267.   What was Steve's last season as a player at White Hart Lane?

268.   Which Cup did Steve win in 1972 and 1984 with Spurs?

269.   Name the "United" that Steve joined when he left Spurs.

270.   What was Steve awarded in 1986 - a CBE, MBE or OBE?

TRIVIA - 4

271. Who became the youngest captain in modern times, aged 20, of Spurs in 1971?

272. This Spurs defender made the 600th senior appearance of his club career in the match against Arsenal on 29 April 1995. Can you name him?

273. Who played his last senior game for Spurs against Arsenal on 8 April 2001?

274. What was Gary Lineker awarded in 1992 - a CBE, MBE or an OBE?

275. Name the famous Spurs captain who managed Chelsea from December 1978 to September 1979.

276. Name the Glasgow Rangers player who was the last player that Bill Nicholson signed for Spurs.

277. What was significant about Roy Low replacing Derek Possee in a match against Arsenal on 11 September 1965?

278. Name the Spurs manager who signed Osvaldo Ardiles and Ricky Villa.

279. Up to May 2004, what is most number of games won by Spurs in a season in the Premier League?

280. Following on from Q279, name any season they achieved this?

SEASON 2001-2002

281.   With which Midlands club did Spurs draw 0-0 at home on the opening day of the season?

282.   How many Premier League games did Spurs win - 13, 14 or 15?

283.   Can you name the "City" Spurs beat 2-0 away in the FA Cup 3rd Round?

284.   Spurs' first win in the League was a 2-1 victory over Southampton at White Hart Lane on 9 September. Name the defender who scored for the second successive game.

285.   Name a London team who Spurs beat in the League Cup.

286.   Spurs led a team 3-0 at half-time in the Premier League on 29 September. Who eventually beat Spurs 5-3?

287.   Following on from Q286, name any Spurs goalscorer in the game.

288.   Can you recall the London club who put Spurs out of the FA Cup?

289.   Apart from the team in Q288, Spurs met the same opposition in the FA Cup and League Cup on 2 other occasions. Name either side.

290.   Which former Spurs manager benefited from the Testimonial Match played at White Hart Lane on 8 August 2001 against Fiorentina?

LEGEND - PAUL GASCOIGNE - 2

291.   When he was an apprentice at Newcastle United, Paul left a
        pair of boots belonging to a 1st team player on the Newcastle
        Underground. Name the owner of the boots.

292.   Can you recall which team Paul was playing for when he
        crashed the team bus at their training ground?

293.   Which club was Paul playing for when he belched into a
        microphone after being approached for an interview?

294.   How many senior appearances did Paul make for Newcastle
        United - 107, 108 or 109?

295.   Which club was Paul playing for when he lifted the yellow card
        dropped by the referee and held it in the air, jokingly booking
        the referee, only for the referee to book him?

296.   Who was Paul's manager at Newcastle United when he made
        his senior debut for the club?

297.   Who were England due to play when Paul was approached by
        a TV crew and asked if he had a message for the people of the
        country only for Gazza to swear at them?

298.   To the nearest 5, how many goals did Paul score for Spurs?

299.   Can you name the Scotland defender that Paul lobbed the ball
        over before scoring at Wembley in Euro 1996?

300.   Following on from Q299, name the player who squirted water
        into Gazza's mouth as he lay on the pitch.

SPURS v ARSENAL - 2

301.   Can you name the Spurs striker who scored in 3 consecutive games against Arsenal between February and March 1987?

302.   What was the score of the Premier League game between the 2 teams at White Hart Lane on 23 November 2004?

303.   Prior to the 2006-2007 season, in what season did Spurs last beat Arsenal in the Premier League?

304.   Name any Spurs goalscorer in Q303.

305.   Up to the end of 2006, who was the last Spurs player to score against Arsenal in an FA Cup tie?

306.   Up to the end of 2006, who was the last player to score a penalty against Arsenal?

307.   Name the "Paul" that was the last Spurs player to score a First Division goal against Arsenal.

308.   In which year did Spurs last meet Arsenal in the FA Charity Shield?

309.   Spurs beat Arsenal 3-1 in the 1991 FA Cup Semi-Final. Paul Gascoigne scored 1 but who scored the other 2?

310.   What was the score of the first meeting between the 2 sides in the Premier League?

SPURS IN THE FA CUP - 1

311.   Which "City" were the first team to beat Spurs in an FA Cup Final?

312.   Which "United" did Spurs beat in 1901 to win the FA Cup for the first time?

313.   Up to 2004, how many times has Spurs won the FA Cup?

314.   True or False: Spurs have won more Cup Finals in a year ending with a "1" than at any other time.

315.   How many times have Spurs finished Runners-Up at Wembley in the FA Cup Final?

316.   Up to 2004, which team were the last team that Spurs met in an FA Cup Final?

317.   On how many occasions were Spurs involved in an FA Cup Final Replay?

318.   Spurs beat this team in an FA Cup Final but were put out of the 1995-96 competition by the same side on penalties. Can you name them?

319.   Who was the last player to captain Spurs to FA Cup success?

320.   Name any team that Spurs have beaten in an FA Cup Final Replay.

LEGEND - PAT JENNINGS

321.   Can you name the "Town" in Northern Ireland where Pat
       started his football career?

322.   From which club did Spurs buy Pat?

323.   Name the legendary Spurs manager who brought Pat to White
       Hart Lane.

324.   To the nearest £5,000, how much did Pat cost Spurs?

325.   Which was the first trophy that Pat won with Spurs?

326.   In which year did Pat join Spurs - 1964, 1965 or 1966?

327.   Against which team did Pat score from his own penalty area in
       the FA Charity Shield?

328.   What award did Pat win in season 1975-1976?

329.   What was the last trophy Pat won with Spurs?

330.   Can you recall the club Pat joined when he first left White
       Hart Lane?

TRIVIA - 5

331. Up to 2004, only 3 players have captained a winning FA Cup side in consecutive years and 2 of them are Spurs heroes. Name them.

332. Can you name the former Spurs hero who was capped by his country 119 times and appeared in 2 World Cup Final tournaments?

333. In which Cup was Spurs' first game in the competition when they played West Herts?

334. Up to and including the 2006 Final, only 2 teams have won the FA Cup more times than Spurs. Name them.

335. Can you name the former Spurs player who was the first England player to be sent off?

336. Which 2004-05 Coca-Cola League Two team links Paul Gascoigne and Howard Wilkinson?

337. In which year did Steve Perryman win his first full England cap - 1980, 1981 or 1982?

338. Can you name the famous Portuguese team that Spurs beat in the Final of the Costa Del Sol Tournament in 1966?

339. What Bundesliga team did Jurgen Klinsmann join in 1984?

340. Up to the end of 2004, how many times has Spurs played Arsenal in the FA Cup - 5, 6 or 7?

FA CUP WINNERS - 1961

341. Can you recall the lower League club that Spurs beat in Round 4?

342. Apart from White Hart Lane, at which other English Football League Division 1 side's ground did Spurs play 2 FA Cup ties?

343. Which North East club did Spurs beat in Round 6?

344. How many of their FA Cup ties went to a Replay?

345. Name the "Allen" who scored 2 goals in Spurs' 3-2 win against Charlton Athletic in the 3rd Round.

346. Who captained Spurs to FA Cup success?

347. Can you recall Spurs' biggest victory on their way to winning the Cup - 5-0, 6-0 or 7-0?

348. Who scored twice for Spurs in the Semi-Final win over Burnley?

349. How many home games did Spurs play in the Cup - 2, 3 or 4?

350. What was the score against Leicester City in the Final?

SEASON 2000-2001

351. What 'Town' did Spurs beat 3-1 at White Hart Lane on the opening day of the season?

352. How many Premier League games did Spurs win - 13, 14 or 15?

353. Can you name the London team that Spurs beat 1-0 away in the FA Cup 3rd Round?

354. Against which "City" did Spurs record their first away win in the League?

355. Name the recent signing who scored twice in only his 4th Premier League game of the season when Spurs beat Everton 3-2 at White Hart Lane.

356. Can you name the "United" Spurs beat 4-2 at White Hart Lane, their best League win of the season?

357. Which "City" put Spurs out of the League Cup?

358. Can you recall the London club that put Spurs out of the FA Cup?

359. Which team did Spurs beat 3-1 at White Hart Lane on the last day of the season?

360. Following on from Q359, can you name the Dutch player who scored Spurs' 1st and 3rd goals in the game?

LEGEND - RAY CLEMENCE

361.   Can you name the club where Ray started his football career?

362.   From which club did Spurs buy Ray?

363.   Name the legendary manager who brought Ray to the club in Q362.

364.   To the nearest £50,000, how much did Ray cost Spurs?

365.   In what year did Ray join Spurs - 1980, 1981 or 1982?

366.   What was the first trophy that Ray won with Spurs?

367.   How many League Championship medals did Ray win with the club in Q362?

368.   To the nearest 30, how many games did Ray play for Spurs?

369.   Under how many different managers did Ray play under at White Hart Lane?

370.   Against which North East club did Ray make his Spurs League debut?

UEFA CUP WINNERS - 1972

371. Which English club did Spurs meet in the Final?

372. Can you recall either the 1st or 2nd Leg scores in the Final?

373. Who scored 2 goals for Spurs in the Final over the 2 Legs?

374. Apart from the player in Q373, name the other Spurs goalscorer in the Final.

375. How many games in total did Spurs play in the 1971-72 UEFA Cup competition?

376. Name any Spurs player who scored a hat-trick in the 1971-72 UEFA Cup competition.

377. Can you recall the French side that Spurs beat 1-0 over 2 Legs in Round 2?

378. Which "Rapid" team did Spurs beat in Round 3?

379. Name the Italian giants that Spurs beat in the Semi-Finals.

380. This young midfielder scored 2 goals in the Semi-Final 1st Leg at White Hart Lane. Name him.

EUROPEAN CUP WINNERS' CUP WINNERS - 1963

381.   Which Spanish club did Spurs meet in the Final?

382.   Can you recall the score in the Final?

383.   2 players scored 2 goals each for Spurs in the Final. Can you name either of the 2?

384.   In which Dutch city was the Final played?

385.   How many games in total did Spurs play in the 1962-63 European Cup Winners' Cup competition?

386.   Name the Scottish club who Spurs beat in Round 2.

387.   Can you recall the "Slovan" team that Spurs beat 6-2 over 2 Legs in the Quarter-Finals?

388.   A player with the same surname as a famous 1994 Blackburn Rovers centre forward scored an own goal playing for the Scottish team in Q386. Can you recall the surname?

389.   In how many games did Spurs fail to score?

390.   This "John" scored in both the Semi-Final and Final. Name him.

TRIVIA - 6

391.   Can you name the Spurs striker from season 1994-1995 who won a bronze medal at the 1988 Olympic Games playing for his country?

392.   Name the Spurs player who retired through injury in March 1988 after more than 300 games for the club plus over 600 games for his previous club.

393.   Who scored Spurs' only goal in the 1971-72 UEFA Cup Quarter-Final tie, which was enough to put them into the Semi-Finals?

394.   Can you recall which Country's managerial award Steve Perryman won in 1999?

395.   In which year did Gary Lineker leave Spurs?

396.   Can you name the former Spurs hero who was the manager of Crystal Palace from 1982 to 1984?

397.   How many goals did Alan Gilzean score for Spurs against Arsenal - 7, 8 or 9?

398.   Who was the chairman of Spurs when Keith Burkinshaw decided to leave the club in May 1984?

399.   Which famous future manager of England did Spurs sign from Southampton for £21,000 in 1949?

400.   Can you name Spurs' Dutch opponents in Round of 32 of the 2006-07 UEFA Cup who Spurs also met in the 1974 final?

SPURS IN THE EUROPEAN CUP

401.   Spurs have only ever participated in the European Cup competition once. Name the season.

402.   Following on from Q401, how far did they progress?

403.   What Polish "Gornik" team was the first team to beat Spurs in a European Cup tie?

404.   How many games in total has Spurs played in the European Cup?

405.   Can you name the Dutch team that Spurs met in the European Cup and at whose stadium they would win 1 of the 3 major European competitions in season 1962-1963?

406.   Can you recall the Portuguese giants that put Spurs out of their inaugural and only European Cup campaign?

407.   Who is the only Spurs player to have scored a penalty in a European Cup tie for the club?

408.   Can you name Spurs' leading goalscorer in the European Cup?

409.   What is the highest number of goals scored by Spurs in a single European Cup tie - 8, 9 or 10?

410.   Which "Prague" did Spurs beat in the European Cup during the season in Q401?

SPURS IN EUROPE

411.   Why did Spurs not participate in the 1961-62 European Cup
        Winners' Cup competition despite winning the FA Cup in 1961?

412.   Which Yugoslavian team did Spurs beat over 2 Legs in the
        1962-63 European Cup Winners' Cup Semi-Finals?

413.   Who scored 2 goals for Spurs in their 3-2 win over Glasgow
        Rangers at Ibrox Stadium in a Round 2, 2nd Leg tie during the
        1962-63 European Cup Winners' Cup?

414.   Who were Spurs' first British opponents in 1 of the 3 major
        European competitions?

415.   From which Eastern European country were Spurs' first ever
        opponents in one of the 3 major European competitions?

416.   Prior to the 2006-2007 season, in what season did Spurs last
        participate in one of the major European competitions?

417.   Following on from Q416, can you name the Cup in which they
        participated?

418.   In which European competition did a Spurs team participate in
        1995?

419.   Prior to the 2006-2007 season, can you recall the German side
        that was the last team Spurs met in one of the major European
        competitions?

420.   Which German team beat Spurs 8-0 in the European
        competition in Q418?

SPURS IN THE UEFA CUP

421. Who scored for Spurs at White Hart Lane in the 1984 UEFA Cup Final?

422. Name the Spurs player who scored against his previous club in Spurs 1-0 third UEFA Cup group game victory durng 2006-07.

423. Which Greek team were the first to beat Spurs in a UEFA Cup match?

424. Can you name any 2 of the 4 teams who along with Spurs made-up Group B in the 2006-07 UEFA Cup?

425. Can you name the Belgian team that Spurs beat in the 1984-85 UEFA Cup?

426. Name Spurs' leading goalscorer in their successful 1983-84 UEFA Cup campaign.

427. Can you name the team Spurs played in Round 1 of the 2006-07 UEFA Cup?

428. From which country were the "Bohemians" that Spurs met in the 1984-85 UEFA Cup?

429. What 'Martin' was the first Spurs player to score 2 hat-tricks for the club in the UEFA Cup?

430. Can you name the English side which put Spurs, the holders, out of the 1972-73 UEFA Cup?

SPURS IN THE EUROPEAN CUP WINNERS' CUP

431. Who were Spurs' first English opponents in 1 of the 3 major European competitions?

432. Which Yugoslav team was the first team to beat Spurs in a European Cup Winners' Cup match?

433. What Portuguese side did Spurs beat in the 1991-92 European Cup Winners' Cup?

434. A future Spurs manager scored in the Spurs v Hajduk Split European Cup Winners' Cup match on 27 September 1967 at White Hart Lane. Name him.

435. Name any Spurs goalscorer from their 1963-64 European Cup Winners' Cup campaign.

436. Which Dutch team were the last team that Spurs played in the European Cup Winners' Cup?

437. Can you name the team that put Spurs, the holders, out of the 1963-64 European Cup Winners' Cup?

438. Name the 'Jimmy' other than Jimmy Greaves who scored 3 goals in Spurs' 1967-68 ECWC campaign.

439. Up to and including the 2006-2007 season, how many times have Spurs been drawn to meet a Northern Irish League team in 1 of the 3 major European competitions?

440. Can you name either of the last 2 players that scored for Spurs in a European Cup Winners' Cup tie?

SPURS IN THE FA CUP - 2

441.   In what famous London stadium did Spurs draw their 1901
        FA Cup Final?

442.   Spurs won their 1901 FA Cup Final Replay at the ground of a
        2004-2005 Lancashire Premier League team. However, the team
        have since moved grounds. Can you name the Park where
        Spurs lifted the FA Cup in 1901?

443.   Up to the 2004 Final, who was the last Spurs manager to win
        the FA Cup?

444.   Can you recall the name of any player that scored for Spurs in
        the 1991 FA Cup Final?

445.   Who was the last Spurs captain to score for the club in an FA
        Cup Final?

446.   Can you name the player who scored for Spurs in both the 1982
        FA Cup Final and the 1982 FA Cup Final Replay?

447.   Name the future BBC Match of the Day reporter who scored for
        Spurs in the 1981 FA Cup Final.

448.   Who was in goal for Spurs in both the 1981 FA Cup Final and
        the 1981 FA Cup Final Replay?

449.   Which club did Spurs beat in the 1981 FA Cup Final?

450.   Following on from Q449, can you name the player who scored
        for both clubs in the Final?

LEAGUE CUP WINNERS - 1999

451.   What Lancashire team did Spurs beat in the 5th Round of the Cup?

452.   What was remarkable about Spurs' victory over the team in Q451?

453.   Name the Runners-Up to Spurs.

454.   Who scored the only goal of the game in the Final?

455.   Can you recall the name of either of the 2 Spurs defenders who scored in the Round 2, 1st Leg win away to Brentford?

456.   Name the Spurs manager who guided the team to victory.

457.   Can you name any 1 of the 4 substitutes that Spurs did not use in the Final?

458.   Who was in goal for Spurs?

459.   Which London club did Spurs beat over 2 Legs in the Semi-Finals?

460.   Who was Spurs' top goalscorer in the competition with 5 goals?

LEGEND - GRAHAM ROBERTS

461.   Can you name the 2004-05 Premier League club where Graham started his football career only to be rejected by them as a schoolboy?

462.   Which Midlands club tried to sign Graham before Spurs did?

463.   Name the non-League club he joined Spurs from.

464.   Which "Paul" was Graham's partner in the heart of the Spurs defence when Spurs won consecutive FA Cups in the 1980s?

465.   In which year did Graham join Spurs - 1979, 1980 or 1981?

466.   What was the first trophy that Graham won with Spurs?

467.   In which Cup Final did Graham captain Spurs to victory?

468.   Can you recall the "Steve" that Spurs bought to replace Graham Roberts?

469.   Name the 3 managers that Graham played under at White Hart Lane.

470.   Which club did he join when he left Spurs?

TRIVIA - 7

471.   Which team put Spurs out of the 2004-05 League Cup on penalties?

472.   Which "City" have Spurs beaten in an FA Cup Final and in a League Cup Final?

473.   Why did Steve Perryman not captain Spurs in the 1984 UEFA Cup Final 2nd Leg?

474.   Can you name the Spurs player from the 1983-1984 season who won 3 European Cup medals?

475.   Name any team that Spurs played in the 1995 Intertoto Cup.

476.   Prior to the 2006-2007 season, who was the last player to score for Spurs in a European tie?

477.   To the nearest 10, how many League goals did Gary Lineker score for Spurs?

478.   In which year did Spurs win the Football League Championship for the first time?

479.   Can you name the former Spurs manager who was the player of Crystal Palace from 1976 to 1980?

480.   Who are the only team to have defeated Spurs in two different European competitions?

SPURS HEROES - 1

481.   What was so sweet personally about Graham Roberts' only hat-trick for Spurs?

482.   Can you name the winger that was the only Spurs substitute that was used from 5 in the 1999 League Cup Final?

483.   Can you name the Spurs player from season 2002-2003 who won a Champions League winners' medal?

484.   Name the only Spurs player to have scored in the 1971-72 UEFA Cup Semi-Final and Final.

485.   At the time, who was Spurs' number 1 goalkeeper but missed out on the 1984 UEFA Cup Final?

486.   Which team did Steve Perryman lead to one 1st-place finishes, one 2nd place and two 3rd places?

487.   How many League games, to the nearest 10, did Gary Lineker play for Spurs?

488.   In which year did Pat Jennings first represent Northern Ireland at the World Cup Finals?

489.   Against which South American country did Jurgen Klinsmann make his full international debut for Germany?

490.   Can you name the "United" that Paul Gascoigne joined in 2004?

OPPONENTS - 1

491.   Why was Spurs' League game against Arsenal at White Hart Lane on 12 October 1940 abandoned after 47 minutes?

492.   What British team, whose name begins and ends with the same letter, did Spurs meet in the 1972-73 UEFA Cup?

493.   Can you name the English team, beginning with the letter "S", that Spurs played in a pre-season friendly 4 years in a row from 2001?

494.   Which club has Spurs beaten in a European Final and in an FA Cup Final?

495.   Can you name the former Chelsea player who scored a hat-trick for Spurs against Chelsea on 15 April 1960?

496.   Up to the end of 2006, how many times have Spurs beaten Arsenal away in the Premier League?

497.   What is Spurs' record away score in Europe - 6-0, 7-0 or 8-0?

498.   Name the player who scored on his debut in the Spurs v Chelsea game on 24 August 1957.

499.   Which team have Spurs beaten in the European Cup, drawn with in the UEFA Cup and lost to in the European Cup Winners' Cup?

500.   Up to and including the 2006-2007 season, name the 2 Scottish teams that Spurs have met in European competition.

DAVID PLEAT

501.   Which club did David Pleat join in 1964?

502.   Can you recall the "Town" he signed for in 1967?

503.   Of which club was he appointed the manager in 1978, succeeding Harry Haslam?

504.   In between the clubs in Q502 and Q503, can you name any 1 of the other 3 clubs he was at?

505.   Which Championship did he lead the team in Q503 to in 1982?

506.   In which year was he first appointed the manager of Spurs - 1984, 1985 or 1986?

507.   Following on from Q506, in which year did his first spell as Spurs manager end?

508.   Following on from Q507, which Greek club offered him a job as their manager after he left Spurs?

509.   Following on from Q507, can you name the "City" that he became the manager of after he left White Hart Lane?

510.   What position did he take up at White Hart Lane in 1998?

LEGEND - OSSIE ARDILES

511. In which year did Ossie win a World Cup Winners' medal with Argentina?

512. What was the first domestic trophy that Ossie won with Spurs?

513. Why did Ossie leave Spurs on 5 April 1982?

514. Can you recall the French side he joined on loan?

515. What was his last match for the club prior to the 1982 World Cup Finals?

516. Which "Town" gave Ossie his first managerial job?

517. Can you recall the name of the club that Ossie managed immediately before he became the Spurs manager?

518. In which year was Ossie appointed the Spurs manager?

519. Name the "County" that beat Spurs in a League Cup game, effectively resulting in Ossie being sacked.

520. In which year did Ossie leave at Spurs manager?

LEGEND - JIMMY GREAVES

521. Which London club was situated closest to where Jimmy grew up?

522. At which club did Jimmy begin his Professional career?

523. Which club did he almost sign for prior to signing for the team in Q522?

524. Name the Italian side he joined in 1960-61.

525. In which year did Jimmy join Spurs?

526. Against which seaside club did Jimmy Greaves make his Spurs debut?

527. How many League goals did Jimmy score in his 22 League appearances for Spurs during the season he joined them?

528. What was the first trophy that Jimmy won with Spurs?

529. In 1962-63 Jimmy set a new record number of League goals scored in a single season by a Spurs player. How many League goals did he score - 37, 38 or 39?

530. Following on from Q529, the previous record was 36 goals in a season and was held jointly by 2 players. Name either of the 2.

TRIVIA - 8

531.   What was Spurs' 1981 FA Cup Final song called?

532.   Following on from Q531, who wrote and sang the song with the Spurs squad?

533.   How many times have Spurs entered 1 of the 3 major European competitions as the Cup holders?

534.   Name the 2 men who have managed both Spurs and England.

535.   Which future Spurs striker scored 114 goals in the 1956-1957 season for his club's Youth Team?

536.   In which year did Gary Lineker win the World Cup Golden Boot Award?

537.   Can you name the famous Italian manager who was Jurgen Klinsmann's manager at Bayern Munich?

538.   Which winger made his 250th appearance for Spurs against Chelsea on 28 October 2000?

539.   Which was Steve Perryman's last Cup Final appearance for Spurs?

540.   Which of the 3 major European competitions did Spurs win first?

LEGEND - CLIVE ALLEN

541.   From which club did Clive join Spurs?

542.   In which year did he sign for Spurs?

543.   Against which Midlands club did Clive score a hat-trick on the opening day of the 1986-1987 season?

544.   How many goals did Clive score in Cup competitions for Spurs in the 1986-1987 season - 16, 17 or 18?

545.   Can you recall the London club who Clive scored a hat-trick against in the Littlewoods Cup (League Cup) during the 1986-1987 season?

546.   How many League goals did Clive score for Spurs in season 1986-1987 - 33, 34 or 35?

547.   In which year did Clive win the Professional Footballers' Association Player of the Year Award?

548.   To the nearest 5, how many League goals did Clive Allen score for Spurs in season 1987-1988?

549.   In which year did Clive leave White Hart Lane?

550.   Following on from Q549, which French League side did he join?

SEASON 2006-07 - 2

551.   Name the England goalkeeper Paul Robinson scored against on St Patrick's Day 2007.

552.   Which club put Spurs out of the Carling Cup in season 2006-07?

553.   Who scored Spurs' first goal of 2007?

554.   Spurs met and beat this "United" in the FA Cup 4th Round. Can you name them or the score of the game?

555.   To the nearest 10 how many goals did Spurs score in all competitions during the 2006-07 season?

556.   Name the two Spurs player who each scored twice in Spurs 4-0 away win over Fulham in the FA Cup 5th Round.

557.   Spurs played two French League teams in a pre-season friendly. Name either 1 of the 2.

558.   Can you name the Lancashire team Spurs beat 2-1 at White Hart Lane on the final day of the 2006-07 Premiership season?

559.   Spurs suffered their first home defeat of 2007 to this "United" in the Premiership. Name the team that won 3-2 at White Hart Lane.

560.   Name the club that knocked Spurs out of the 2006-07 FA Cup in the quarter-finals.

SPURS v ARSENAL - THE FACTS

561.   What is Spurs' biggest home win over Arsenal - 5-0, 6-0 or 7-0?

562.   Can you recall Spurs' biggest away win - 3-0, 4-0 or 5-0?

563.   What is Spurs' heaviest home defeat to Arsenal - 5-0, 6-0 or 7-0?

564.   Can you recall the biggest away defeat - 5-0, 6-0 or 7-0?

565.   What is the highest number of goals scored in a game involving the 2 teams?

566.   To the nearest 5,000, what is Spurs' biggest home crowd with Arsenal as the visitors?

567.   To the nearest 5,000, what is the record attendance for the 2 clubs in a game at Arsenal?

568.   Can you name either the competition or the year when the highest ever crowd attendance involving the 2 teams was set?

569.   What is the longest run of games between the 2 sides without a goal being scored by either team?

570.   Can you recall Spurs' longest sequence of games without losing to Arsenal?

TRIVIA - 9

571.   3 players from Argentina's 1978 World Cup winning squad played for Spurs sometime during their career. Name all 3.

572.   Which Serie A team did Spurs play for Ossie Ardiles' Testimonial?

573.   Following on from Q571, which former Arsenal player played against Spurs in the game?

574.   Name the Spurs player who later managed Wimbledon in the Premier League.

575.   Can you name the Belgian player who played for Spurs whose full name both begins and ends with the same letter?
       (For example: Sean Collins.)

576.   Name the last player to score for England, excluding a penalty shoot-out, when Terry Venables was the manager?

577.   Name the future Spurs player that scored for Germany against England in the Euro'96 Semi-Final penalty shoot-out at Wembley.

578.   What was so unusual about Spurs' 2-0 home defeat to Leicester City on 3 April 1999?

579.   Only 1 Spurs player scored a hat-trick in a competitive fixture during the 1998-1999 season. Can you recall who it was?

580.   At which London ground did Spurs play their 1981 FA Cup Semi-Final Replay?

SPURS HEROES - 2

581.   Four players have played in a World Cup Final and also
       featured in the League for Spurs. Name any three of the four.

582.   Can you name the player who signed for Spurs on 1 August
       1979 and who both played for and managed Wales?

583.   Can you name the former Northern Ireland international who
       played for Spurs whose full name both begins and ends with
       the same letter? *(For example: Sean Collins.)*

584.   Who scored in 3 consecutive games for Spurs against
       Nottingham Forest, West Ham United and Manchester United
       in season 1998-1999?

585.   Name the former Scottish defender who played for Spurs and
       whose first name and Surname begin with the letter "C".

586.   Name the Spurs player who scored twice for England against
       Hungary at Wembley in a 3-0 win on 18 May 1996.

587.   Who in 1982 became the only Spurs player to score for Scotland
       at the World Cup Finals?

588.   Can you name the Spurs midfielder who scored 12 League
       goals in season 1980-1981?

589.   Name the early 1980s Spurs striker who scored 75 goals in 182
       appearances for the club over 5 years.

590.   He played 7 World Cup Final stage games for England in 1962
       and 1966, scoring 1 goal. Who is he?

OPPONENTS - 2

591.   Spurs played Anderlect in the 1984 UEFA Cup Final, but which English team did they beat in the semi-final?

592.   Which International team did Spurs play in Keith Burkinshaw's Testimonial?

593.   Which team did Spurs play against 6 times during the 1998-1999 season?

594.   Can you recall the name of the Lancashire club who Spurs beat in their last game of 1998?

595.   Name the club who were the first team that Spurs drew 0-0 with in all competitions during the 1998-1999 season.

596.   Which team did Spurs beat to win the 100th FA Cup Final?

597.   Name the team that Spurs drew 2-2 with to share the 1981 FA Charity Shield.

598.   Which team did Spurs beat in the 1986-87 FA Cup Semi-Final?

599.   Against which "City" did Clive Allen score a hat-trick in the 1986-1987 season?

600.   Can you recall the Midlands club who Spurs recorded their biggest Premier League win against during the 2003-2004 season?

MARTIN JOL

601.   Where in Holland was Martin born - Amsterdam, Den Haag or Rotterdam?

602.   At which Dutch club did he begin his Professional career?

603.   Which award did Martin win in 1987?

604.   Which Midlands club did he join in 1981?

605.   Can you recall the English "City" that he played for between 1984 and 1985?

606.   What is Martin's nickname at Spurs?

607.   Which "Football Writers" award did he win in 2001?

608.   Who did he succeed as the manager of Spurs?

609.   Name the club Martin was linked with a management switch to in early 2005.

610.   Can you name the FA Premier League club who was reportedly interested in signing Martin as a No.2 to their current manager before he elected to join Spurs?

EDGAR DAVIDS

611.   In which South American country was Edgar born?

612.   At what Dutch club did Edgar begin his professional career?

613.   Name the manager who brought Edgar to White Hart Lane.

614.   From which Italian Serie A side did Spurs sign Edgar?

615.   To the nearest £500,000 how much did Spurs pay for Edgar?

616.   Can you recall the North East club against which Edgar made his FA Premier League debut for Spurs?

617.   Name the club Edgar signed for on 1st October 1997 from AC Milan.

618,   Which country did Edgar play for at international level?

619.   During the 2003-04 season Edgar was on loan at a Spanish club. Name the club.

620.   How many FA Premier League goals did Edgar score for Spurs in his first season at the club?

STRANGE BUT TRUE

621.   Name the legendary Liverpool captain, and winner of countless trophies, who began his football career as an apprentice at Spurs, making only 1 substitute appearance in 1971?

622.   What was significant about Walter Tull's debut for Spurs?

623.   At which stadium have Spurs both won and lost a European Final?

624.   Which former Premier League manager was Spurs' leading goalscorer in the 1978-1979 season?

625.   Can you name the manager whose first game in charge of the club he would later lead to European glory was a 1-0 away win at Spurs in the FA Cup 3rd Round Replay in 1975?

626.   What "first" was the game between Spurs and Nottingham Forest on 2 October 1983?

627.   Can you name the former Spurs apprentice striker (18 games, 4 goals: 1980-83) who was Barnet's Youth Team manager under Ray Clemence.

628.   Can you name the Spurs striker who scored in the 1984 UEFA Cup Final penalty shoot-out and never played for the club again?

629.   Up to the end of 2006, only 1 player has ever been capped by his country, Nigeria, whilst at Spurs. Name him.

630.   Can you name the former Spurs manager who was the youngest player to appear for Nottingham Forest as a 17-year-old in 1962?

PAST MASTERS

631. Who was the regular penalty taker for Spurs during the 1998-1999 season, scoring 3 times?

632. Can you name the overseas Spurs midfielder who scored 8 League goals in season 1981-1982?

633. Who was Spurs' leading goalscorer in the 1979-1980 season?

634. Can you name the striker who scored both of Spurs' goals against Aston Villa in the 1981 FA Charity Shield?

635. Can you name the Spurs striker that had a fall-out with manager Keith Burkinshaw in the 1983-1984 season and was subsequently dropped for a number of games?

636. Name the player whose £35,000 transfer fee was a non-League record when he signed for Spurs in 1980?

637. Can you name the Spurs striker from season 1984-1985 whose Father was a member of Spurs' Double Winners in 1960-61?

638. Name the player who scored a hat-trick for Spurs when he made his debut for the club during the 1961-1962 season.

639. Who was Spurs' leading goalscorer in the 1971-72 UEFA Cup competition?

640. Can you name the former Chelsea player who scored 12 goals for Spurs against Chelsea during his time at White Hart Lane?

SPURS AT THE WORLD CUP - 1

ALL YOU HAVE TO DO HERE IS NAME THE PLAYER

641.   This England player played 4 games at the 1998 World Cup Finals.

642.   I played 7 games in total for England at the 1982 and 1986 World Cup Finals without scoring.

643.   I am a Romanian who played for my country at the 1990, 1994 and 1998 World Cup Finals - 8 games and 2 goals.

644.   I played in the 1986 and 1990 World Cup Finals scoring 10 goals from 12 games.

645.   I played twice for my country at the 1978 World Cup Finals but did not score.

646.   I played 3 games for England in the 1950 World Cup Finals without scoring.

647.   This player scored 3 times in 8 games at the 1986 and 1990 World Cup Finals.

648.   He represented Scotland in the 1986 and 1990 World Cup Finals, playing 4 times.

649.   I played 5 times for Northern Ireland in the 1958 World Cup Finals.

650.   This Norwegian international made 3 appearances at the 1994 World Cup Finals.

SOUNDS LIKE

*ALL YOU HAVE TO DO HERE IS IDENTIFY THE
PAST/PRESENT PLAYER FROM THE CLUES GIVEN*

651. Prolific Spurs striker from the 1980s whose surname sounds like a first name.

652. This England "Bert" sounds very happy.

653. This "Anthony" sounds like he should be doing some work outside the house.

654. Regal sounding Spurs defender from season 2004-2005.

655. This midfielder may have felt quite at home with Robin Hood in the forest.

656. This full back's surname is a mode of transport.

657. Scottish forward whose surname is a South American country.

658. Could he be related to "Bamber" from University Challenge?

659. This 2004-05 player's surname sounds like a Scot who refuses to gamble.

660. A Welsh defender who sounds more English than Welsh.

TERRY VENABLES

661.   In which year was Terry appointed the manager of Spurs?

662.   Can you recall the Lancashire club that beat Spurs 2-0 at White Hart Lane in his first game in charge?

663.   Name the "County" that Spurs recorded their first win against under Terry.

664.   Following on from Q663, name any Spurs goalscorer from the game.

665.   For how many League games was Terry in charge of Spurs - 137, 147 or 157?

666.   What was the total number of games won by Spurs under his management - 58, 68 or 78?

667.   In which year did Terry end his spell as Spurs manager?

668.   Can you recall Spurs' opponents for Terry's last game in charge?

669.   Who was the last player to score for Spurs when Terry was manager - Hendry, Nayim or Lineker?

670.   Against which south coast club did Spurs record their last League win under Terry's management?

TRIVIA - 10

671. In aid of what "Disaster Fund" did Spurs play Arsenal on 29 April 1912?

672. Which Spurs manager signed Jimmy Greaves for the club?

673. Which was Sergei Rebrov's first season at Spurs?

674. Name the defender who was the regular penalty taker for Spurs in season 1988-1989.

675. Can you name the former Blackburn Rovers player who scored his last goal for Spurs against Chelsea on 23 January 2002?

676. How many goals did Paul Gascoigne score for England in full internationals- 10, 11 or 12?

677. What Dutch player was signed from Vitesse Arnhem during 1999?

678. Who joined Spurs from Chelsea in a transfer deal worth £80,000 in May 1966?

679. Which "Cliff" scored 11 goals for Spurs against Chelsea during his time at the club?

680. Apart from Spurs, which other club did David Pleat manage twice?

CAPPED AT SPURS

ALL YOU HAVE TO DO HERE IS NAME THE PLAYER WHO BECAME THE FIRST SPURS PLAYER TO WIN A CAP WITH THE COUNTRY NAMED

681.   South Africa

682.   Sweden

683.   Switzerland

684.   USA

685.   Portugal

686.   Yugoslavia

687.   Iceland

688.   Israel

689.   Argentina

690.   Algeria

LEGEND - STEVE ARCHIBALD

691.   In which year did Steve join Spurs?

692.   Can you recall the Scottish club Steve joined Spurs from?

693.   To the nearest £100,000, how much did Steve cost Spurs?

694.   How many League goals did he score in his first season at White Hart Lane - 20, 22 or 24?

695.   Against which Midlands club did Steve score in Spurs' 1981 FA Cup Semi-Final 2-2 draw?

696.   How many League goals did Steve score in 27 appearances during the 1981-1982 season - 6, 8 or 10?

697.   Who was Steve's strike partner at Spurs in his first season at the club?

698.   In which year did Steve leave Spurs?

699.   Which team did Steve join when he left White Hart Lane?

700.   Can you recall the Scottish club who Steve was the manager of during his career?

ODDS AND ENDS

701.   Can you name the South American side Spurs drew 2-2 with on 15th July 2005?

702.   From which club did Spurs purchase Dimitar Berbatov?

70.3   Name any player who scored for Spurs in the FA Cup during the 2005-06 season.

704.   To the nearest £2.5million, how much did Spurs receive from Manchester United for Michael Carrick?

705.   He scored Spurs last goal of the 2005-06 season. Name him.

706.   In what position in the FA Premier League did Spurs finish for season 2005-06?

707.   Name the 2 Spurs goal scorers in their 2-1 win over Chelsea on 5th November 2006.

708.   Can you recall the team Spurs beat 5-0 in Round 2 of the 2006-07 League Cup?

709.   Who did Martin Jol purchase in 2006 for £10.9 million?

710.   Can you name the sponsor's name, not shirt manufacturer, that appears on the Spurs shirt in season 2006-07?

THE MANAGEMENT GAME

711. Can you name the former Spurs manager who played for Exeter City against Manchester United, the current European Champions, in the FA Cup on 4 January 1969?

712. Name the Spurs manager who won the Dutch Cup as a player in 1976.

713. To the nearest 5, how many caps did Spurs' sporting director, Frank Arnesen, win?

714. Can you name the Spurs player who was signed as a Professional by the club in 1929 and later became the first Spurs manager to win the Football League Championship?

715. Three men have both played for and managed Spurs since Bill Nicholson was in charge at White Hart Lane (excluding a caretaker position). Name them.

716. From which club did Keith Burkinshaw sign Alan Brazil in early 1983?

717. Name the 'Town' that was managed by 2 future Spurs managers during the late1980s/early1990s.

718. Can you name the former Spurs captain who managed Start FC in Norway from 1994 to 1995?

719. Who is the only Spurs manager to have both played for and managed Arsenal?

720. Can you name the club who David Pleat led to a 7th place finish in the Premier League in season 1996-1997?

LEGEND - GARTH CROOKS

721.   In what year did Garth join Spurs?

722.   Garth was the top goalscorer at his previous club the year before he signed for Spurs. Can you name the club?

723.   How many League goals did Garth score for Spurs in his first season at White Hart Lane - 14, 15 or 16?

724.   To the nearest £100,000, how much did Spurs pay for Garth?

725.   Name either of the 2 important games in which Garth scored for Spurs in season 1980-1981.

726.   Can you recall the Midlands club who Garth scored a bullet of a header against in a 6-1 win for Spurs in 1981-1982?

727.   Which team did Garth join on loan for a while in season 1983-1984?

728.   How many goals did he score in 22 League games during the 1984-1985 season?

729.   What was the highest consecutive number of League games that Garth scored in during the 1984-1985 season, including a goal against Arsenal in a 2-1 win on New Year's Day?

730.   Upon leaving White Hart Lane, which Midlands club did he join?

TERRY VENABLES - ENGLAND MANAGER

731. England's first away game under Terry was in Dublin against the Republic of Ireland on 15 February 1995. What happened that spoilt the occasion?

732. Against which Scandinavian country did England record their first victory under Terry?

733. Which sports manufacturer sponsored Cup Tournament did England host in the summer of 1995?

734. Name 2 of the 3 countries that England played in Q733.

735. Following on from Q733, apart from Wembley where else did England play a game in the competition?

736. Name the defender who Terry gave his full England debut to as a substitute versus Portugal at Wembley in 1995?

737. Name either of the 2 Spurs players who Terry gave their England debuts to as substitutes in the 3-0 win over Hungary in 1996.

738. What was significant about 2 debut caps awarded by Terry to 2 Manchester United players against China in Beijing in 1996?

739. In the Euro'96 Semi-Final, England drew 1-1 with Germany at Wembley. Can you name the scorer of the German equaliser.

740. Name the Colombian goalkeeper who made a scorpion kick-save from Jamie Redknapp at Wembley in 1995.

SEASON 1999 - 2000

741.   Which London team did Spurs lose 1-0 to on the opening day of the season?

742.   How many Premier League games did Spurs win - 13, 14 or 15?

743.   Can you name the team who Spurs lost 6-1 away to in their FA Cup 3rd Round Replay?

744.   Against which "United" did Spurs record their first win in the League?

745.   Name the midfielder who scored in 3 of Spurs' opening 5 League games of the season.

746.   Spurs played 3 "Citys" from 12 September to 3 October in the League, winning against 1, drawing with 1 and losing to 1. Which "City" did they beat?

747.   What London club brought an end to Spurs' reign as League Cup holders?

748.   Can you name the Spurs player who scored against his former club in the FA Cup?

749.   Name the Spurs striker who scored a hat-trick against GAIS in a pre-season friendly.

750.   To which team did Spurs lose their last away game of the season for the second successive year?

TRIVIA - 11

751.   Name the Spurs manager who led his former team from the 3rd Division of their League to the 1st Division between 1991 and 1995.

752.   Can you name a Spurs goalkeeper whose full name both begins and ends with the same letter? *(For example: Sean Collins.)*

753.   2 players named "Alan" played for Spurs in the 1967 FA Cup Final. Name them both.

754.   Can you recall the Liverpool defender who scored an own goal in both Premier League games against Spurs in season 1998-1999?

755.   I played for Spurs, Coventry City, Manchester United, Swindon Town and Wimbledon. Who am I?

756.   How many League goals did Spurs score in season 1980-1981 - 50, 60 or 70?

757.   Name the 1980's Spurs striker who scored 78 goals in 189 appearances for the club over 4 years.

758.   Who was the first non-British player to score for Spurs in a major Cup Final?

759.   This Northern Ireland Spurs international striker scored 4 League goals in 30 games during the 1979-1980 season. Name him.

760.   Can you name the South American country who Darren Anderton scored for England against in the 1998 World Cup Finals?

FA CUP WINNERS - 1981

761. Which London club did Spurs beat in the 3rd Round Replay?

762. Name any 1 of the 3 goalscorers from the game in Q761.

763. Name the lower Division "City" that Spurs beat in the 4th Round.

764. Who was the Spurs manager that led the team to FA Cup success?

765. Spurs beat a club in the Semi-Final that they had previously beaten in a European Final. Name them.

766. How many goals did Ricky Villa score in the competition?

767. Who, with 4 goals, was Spurs' leading goalscorer in the competition?

768. What was the score in the Final?

769. Spurs beat a "City" in the 6th Round that a future Spurs manager once played for. Name either the "City" or the future Spurs Manager.

770. How many games did Spurs draw in the 1980-81 FA Cup?

SPURS AT THE WORLD CUP - 2

ALL YOU HAVE TO DO HERE IS NAME THE PLAYER

771.   He played for England in 1998 and scored against a South American country.

772.   A Romanian player from the 1990, 1994 and 1998 World Cups with 8 games and 0 goals.

773.   This England player played 11 times in 1986 and 1990 but never scored.

774.   An England player who played 6 games at the 1998 World Cup Finals without finding the net.

775.   He scored for England against Argentina at the 1962 Finals.

776.   This player was an unused England substitute in Spain in the 1982 Finals.

777.   A Scottish player who played 1 game for his country in the 1958 Finals.

778.   He scored for his country against France, Iraq and the Soviet Union at the 1986 Finals.

779.   He played 4 games at the 2002 Finals, scoring 3 times.

780.   He scored a hat-trick against Poland in 1986.

LEGEND - GARY MABBUTT

781. At which "Rovers" did Gary begin his Professional career?

782. Which country's successful team that bid to stage the 2010 World Cup Finals was he a member of?

783. How many full international England caps did Gary win - 14, 15 or 16?

784. Which "Panel" did Gary become a member of in 2002?

785. In which year did he captain Spurs to FA Cup success?

786. Can you recall the "illness" that Gary had to fight constantly during his playing career?

787. Name the West Ham United player that Gary idolised as a boy?

788. What was the first trophy that Gary won with Spurs?

789. Can you recall the Liverpool manager who tried to sign Gary when his Spurs contract ran out in 1987?

790. Name the striker whose elbow almost rearranged Gary's face during a game.

OPPONENTS - 3

791. How many "Citys" did Spurs beat to win the FA Cup in 1981?

792. Against which London club did Spurs record their biggest win, 6-2, during 1997-98?

793. Name either team who Spurs recorded their biggest win against during 1998-99.

794. Which London team beat Spurs in the League Cup Semi-Final during the 1986-1987 season?

795. Name the "United" who were managed by Ossie Ardiles during the early 1990s.

796. What is Spurs' record score in Europe - 8-0, 9-0 or 10-0?

797. Against what "City" did Spurs record their biggest win, 5-1, during 1992-93?

798. From which Dutch club did Spurs sign Willem Korsten?

799. For which club did Gary Lineker score the most goals in his career?

800. Against which "United" did Spurs record their biggest win during 2000-2001?

SEASON 1998-1999

801. Against which London team did Spurs lose 3-1 on the opening day of the season?

802. Which Yorkshire club did Spurs lose 3-0 to in their first home game?

803. Did Les Ferdinand, Ruel Fox or Steffen Iversen score Spurs' first goal of the season?

804. Against which Lancashire club did Spurs record their first win in the League?

805. Spurs lost the last game of the season to the Champions. Name them.

806. Spurs played this London team in 3 consecutive games between 16 January and 27 January. Can you name them?

807. Name the former Liverpool defender who scored against Liverpool in Spurs' 4th Round 3-1 Worthington Cup victory at Anfield.

808. Who scored a spectacular goal against Barnsley in a 1-0 FA Cup 6th Round tie?

809. Name the team who beat Spurs in the FA Cup Semi-Final.

810. In Round 3 of the Worthington Cup, Spurs played a team whose name starts and ends with the same letter. Can you name them?

SPURS v ARSENAL - 3

811.   Who scored Spurs' first goal against Arsenal in the Premier
         League on 12 December 1992?

812.   Up to the end of 2006, who was the last Spurs player to score
         against Arsenal in consecutive League games?

813.   Spurs beat Arsenal 5-0 at White Hart Lane in a First Division
         game on 4 April 1983. Name any Spurs goalscorer.

814.   Name the Spurs favourite who scored in a 1-0 home win over
         Arsenal in a League Cup tie on 4 November 1980.

815.   Which winger scored Spurs' goal in a 3-1 Premier League loss
         at Arsenal on 24 November 1996?

816.   Who scored for Spurs in a 1-1 Premier League draw at Arsenal
         on 29 April 1995?

817.   Name the Belgian player who scored for Spurs in a 2-1 loss at
         Arsenal in the First Division on 18 October 1987.

818.   Which 'Gary' scored in a 1-0 home win over Arsenal in 1986?

819.   Who scored for Spurs against Arsenal in both the First Division
         and in the FA Cup in 1982?

820.   Name either of the Spurs goalscorers in the 2-1 win over
         Arsenal in the Premier League in 1995.

LEGEND - MARTIN CHIVERS

821.   In which year did Martin sign for Spurs - 1966, 1967 or 1968?

822.   From which south coast club did Spurs purchase Martin?

823.   As a future successor to which Spurs legend was Martin bought?

824.   Against which Yorkshire club did he score in his debut for Spurs?

825.   Can you name the Midlands club he scored his first hat-trick for Spurs against?

826.   Who was Martin's strike partner at Spurs in 1970-1971?

827.   When Martin made his full international appearance for England in 1971, which future winners of the European Football Championships did he play against?

828.   Did Martin make 17, 18 or 19 full international appearances for England's Under-23 team?

829.   Against which Scottish "Athletic" team did Martin score a hat-trick in the 1970-1971 Texaco Cup?

830.   When Martin left Spurs he joined a Swiss team. Can you name them?

LEGEND - RICKY VILLA

831.   In which year did Ricky sign for Spurs?

832.   In which city was Ricky born?

833.   Against which club did Ricky make his Spurs debut - Arsenal, Manchester United or Nottingham Forest?

834.   Can you name the year in which Ricky retired from playing professional football- 1986, 1987 or 1988?

835.   Which Miami-based team did he sign for when he left Spurs?

836.   Following on from Q835, which "Deportivo" did he join after leaving this team?

837.   To the nearest 20, how many League appearances did he make for Spurs?

838.   How many League goals did Ricky score for Spurs - 17, 18 or 19?

839.   Which season was Ricky's most successful at White Hart Lane in terms of goals scored?

840.   What was the first domestic trophy he won with Spurs?

TRIVIA - 12

841. How many League goals did Spurs score in season 1979-1980 - 48, 50 or 52?

842. Name any country which Robbie Keane scored for Ireland against in the 2002 World Cup Finals.

843. Which Spurs manager signed Nico Claesen after the Belgian impressed him in the 1986 World Cup Finals?

844. Who arrived at Spurs in 1968 for a then British record fee of £125,000?

845. Can you name the Spurs player who scored a deflected goal in both the Semi-Final and Final of the 1987 FA Cup?

846. Name the former Liverpool striker who played for Spurs and whose first name and surname both begin with the letter "R".

847. Can you name the non-British player who was Spurs' second-highest goalscorer in the League behind Clive Allen with 8 goals in season 1986-1987?

848. To the nearest £50,000, for how much did Spurs sell Graham Roberts to Glasgow Rangers?

849. Which team did Gary Lineker captain from 1990 to 1992?

850. To the nearest 50, how many senior appearances did Steve Perryman make for Spurs?

I PLAYED FOR SPURS & ARSENAL

851.   Up to the end of 2006, who was the last player to leave Arsenal for Spurs?

852.   Can you name the player who joined Spurs from Arsenal in a free transfer in 1985?

853.   Name the "Willie" who left White Hart Lane for Arsenal in March 1977.

854.   Can you name the "Narada" who joined Arsenal from Spurs in July 1999?

855.   This colourful sounding David was the first player to move from White Hart Lane to Arsenal. Name him.

856.   Who is the only player to have left Spurs for Arsenal only to later rejoin Spurs?

857.   To the nearest £25,000, how much is the largest transfer fee involving a player moving between the 2 clubs?

858.   Who played for one club from 1966 until 1972 and later managed the other?

859.   To the nearest £250,000, how much did Spurs receive from Arsenal for Sol Campbell?

860.   Apart from the player in Q853, 2 other players left Spurs and signed for Arsenal in 1977 (August). Can you name either of them?

SPURS v WEST HAM UNITED

861.   Who has scored the most career goals for Spurs against West
        Ham United?

862.   Up to the end of 2006, who was the last player to join West Ham
        United from Spurs?

863.   Up to the end of 2006, who was the last player to join Spurs from
        West Ham United?

864.   To the nearest £500,000, how much did Spurs pay West Ham
        United for Jermain Defoe?

865.   Following on from Q864, which Spurs player joined West Ham
        United as part of the deal?

866.   Who in April 1992 was the last Spurs player to score a hat-trick
        against West Ham United in the League?

867.   How many goals did Vivian Woodward score for Spurs against
        West Ham United on 9 January 1905?

868.   What is Spurs' biggest home win over West Ham United -
        9-0, 10-0 or 11-0?

869.   What is Spurs' biggest away win over West Ham United -
        6-1, 7-1 or 8-1?

870.   Can you name the Spurs striker who scored a hat-trick against
        West Ham United on 2 February 1987?

LEAGUE CUP WINNERS - 1971

871.   Which Welsh "City" did Spurs beat in Round 2?

872.   Name the "Martin" who scored a hat-trick in Round 4.

873.   Against which Midlands club did the player in Q872 score his hat-trick?

874.   Can you name the "City", and future FA Cup Final opponents of Spurs, that Spurs beat in Round 5?

875.   Which "Martin" scored a hat-trick in the game in Q874?

876.   Name the Yorkshire "United" who Spurs beat in Round 3.

877.   Can you recall the "City" that Spurs beat in the Semi-Final?

878.   Spurs beat the inaugural winners of the League Cup in the 1971 Final. Can you name them?

879.   Who scored both of Spurs' goals in their 2-0 Final win?

880.   Which "Alan" scored in the 4th Round, 5th Round and Semi-Final?

LEGEND - MARTIN PETERS

881.   From which club did Spurs sign Martin?

882.   In which year did he arrive at White Hart Lane?

883.   Where was Martin born - London, Manchester or Nottingham?

884.   Against which "City" did Martin score on his debut for Spurs?

885.   Which was the first trophy that Martin won with Spurs?

886.   Can you name the French club who Martin scored against in the 1971-72 UEFA Cup?

887.   How many goals did Martin score for Spurs in the 1973-1974 season - 24, 25 or 26?

888.   To the nearest 25, how many appearances did Martin make for Spurs including friendly matches?

889.   To the nearest 10, how many goals did he score for Spurs?

890.   Which "City" did Martin join when he left White Hart Lane?

TRIVIA - 13

891.   Who scored both of Spurs' goals in their 2-2 draw with Manchester United in the FA Cup in 1968?

892.   Against what "City" did Spurs record their biggest win during 1994-95?

893.   Which number shirt did Graham Roberts normally wear playing in central defence?

894.   Which Spurs player did Sir Alf Ramsey once describe as being "10 years ahead of his time"?

895.   To the nearest 5, how many full international caps did Steve Perryman win for England?

896.   Name the player who scored his only goal for Spurs against West Ham United in 2003 and later joined that team.

897.   Can you name the Spurs player from the 1980s who won the PFA and Football Writers' Player of the Year awards?

898.   To the nearest £25,000, how much did Spurs pay for Alfie Conn?

899.   In which year did Gary Lineker win the European Cup Winners' Cup with Barcelona?

900.   Which Spurs manager signed Willem Korsten?

FA CUP WINNERS - 1982

901.   Why could Spurs not be drawn against the holders of the FA Cup when the 3rd Round draw was made?

902.   Can you recall the London club that Spurs beat 1-0 at White Hart Lane in the 3rd Round?

903.   He scored in the 3rd Round, 4th Round and Semi-Final. Name him.

904.   In the Semi-Final, Spurs beat a team they had previously beaten in an FA Cup Final. Name the team concerned.

905.   Which team did Spurs beat in the Final after a Replay?

906.   Following on from Q905, who scored for Spurs in both the Final and the Final Replay?

907.   Which "United" did Spurs beat in the 4th Round?

908.   Can you recall the London club that Spurs beat 3-2 in the 6th Round?

909.   Apart from Glenn Hoddle, name any other Spurs goalscorer in the game in Q908.

910.   Against which Midlands club did Mark Falco score the only goal of the game in the 5th Round?

LEGEND - GLENN HODDLE

911.   In which year did Glenn make his first team debut for Spurs?

912.   How old was Glenn when he made his debut in Q911?

913.   How many goals did he score for the first team in his first season at White Hart Lane - 1, 3 or 5?

914.   Can you recall the "City" that Glenn made his Spurs debut against?

915.   Against which Lancashire club did he score his first FA Cup goal?

916.   What was the first domestic trophy that Glenn won with Spurs?

917.   Which French club did Glenn join after he left Spurs?

918.   At which club did he begin his managerial career?

919.   Which club did he manage after leaving the team in Q918?

920.   In which year was he appointed the England manager?

LONDON DERBIES

921. Which player scored a brace in the 5-1 Premier League win in December 2006 against Charlton Athletic?

922. How many London Derbies did Spurs play in the Premier League in season 2003-2004?

923. Following on from Q922, how many did they draw?

924. Can you recall the only London team which Spurs beat in season 2003-2004?

925. Name any 4 teams that Spurs played a London Derby against in the Premier League in season 2002-2003.

926. With which team did Spurs draw both their London Derby Premier League games in season 2002-2003?

927. Against which team did Spurs play their last London Derby game of 2004?

928. Against which team did Spurs play their first London Derby game of 2005?

929. Who did Spurs beat 6-2 away in a London Derby game on 2 May 1998?

930. Following on from Q929, who scored 4 goals for Spurs in the game?

LEGEND - ALAN MULLERY

931.   At which London club did Alan begin his Professional career?

932.   In which year did he join Spurs - 1963, 1964 or 1965?

933.   When Alan signed for Spurs it was for a British record transfer fee for a midfield player at the time. To the nearest £10,000 how much did he cost Spurs?

934.   What was the first domestic trophy that Alan won with Spurs?

935.   Can you recall the football award he won in 1975?

936.   How many full international England caps did Alan win during his career - 35, 45 or 55?

937.   In which year did he play for England at the World Cup Finals?

938.   Which club did Alan join when he left White Hart Lane?

939.   Can you recall the last Final that Alan appeared in during his Professional career?

940.   What award did Alan receive in 1976 in recognition of his services to football?

TRIVIA - 14

941. Who took the penalty against Pat Jennings when the ball first hit the post, then flew over the other side of the goal and hit the other post before hitting Pat on the back of the head and going into the empty goal?

942. Can you name the player who scored in Spurs' last 3 Premier League games during the 1997-1998 season?

943. Who, after 5 years at the club, left Spurs in March 1975 in a £50,000 transfer deal?

944. What was the longest run of games in all competitions in which Clive Allen failed to score for Spurs during the 1986-1987 season?

945. Which famous BBC reporter once said, "For those of you watching in black and white, Spurs are in the yellow strip"?

946. Prior to Glenn Hoddle, who was the last Spurs manager to have played for Chelsea?

947. To the nearest 5, how many goals did Paul Gascoigne score for Newcastle United?

948. Can you name the European player who scored his last goal for Spurs against Chelsea on 23 January 2002?

949. Which defender made his 50th appearance for Spurs against Chelsea on 3 April 2004?

950. Can you name the Spurs player who scored in successive FA Cup Finals for the club?

JUANDE RAMOS

951. Can you name the Spanish club beginning with the letter "E" where Juande began his playing career?

952. Aprt from his first club can you name any other club Juande played for?

953. In which position did Juande play during his professional career?

954. Can you name one of hios former clubs that gave him his first taste of management in 1993?

955. In his first season as the manager of Sevilla he guided them to Uefa Cup succeess. Which team did they beat in the 2006 Uefa Cup Final?

956. Juande's Sevilla side won the 2006 European Super Cup but can you name the team they defeated in the Final?

957. Can you name the Premier League club he was linked with the manager's job with in June 2007, a post subsequently filled by a former international manager?

958. Juande began his tenure as Spurs manager with a 2-0 win. Who did Spurs beat?

959. Name the former Spurs player Juande appointed as his assistant when he took charge of Spurs.

960. Juande was unbeaten in his first 6 games in charge of Spurs until they were surprisingly beaten at White Hart Lane. Who beat them?

LEAGUE CUP WINNERS - 1973

961.   Which Yorkshire "Town" did Spurs beat in Round 2?

962.   Can you name the North East club that Spurs played 3 times in the 1972-1973 League Cup?

963.   Excluding the Final, how many away games did Spurs play in the competition?

964.   Can you name the Midlands club who Spurs beat in the Semi-Final?

965.   Which "Martin" scored in both Legs against the team in Q964?

966.   Name the Lancashire club that Spurs beat after a Replay in the 5th Round.

967.   Can you recall the London club that Spurs beat in Round 4?

968.   Which team did Spurs beat in the 1973 Final?

969.   Who scored Spurs' only goal in their 1-0 Final win?

970.   Who was Spurs' top goalscorer in the 1972-1973 League Cup competition?

FA CUP WINNERS - 1967

971.   Which team did Spurs beat in the Final?

972.   Can you recall the score of the Final?

973.   Name the future European Cup winners that Spurs beat in the Semi-Final.

974.   Which London club did Spurs beat after a Replay in the 3rd Round?

975.   Can you name the player, and future manager of a winning FA Cup team, who scored twice for Spurs in their 6th Round Replay win?

976.   Name the Midlands club who Spurs beat in Q975.

977.   Who was Spurs' leading goalscorer in the 1966-67 FA Cup?

978.   Can you name the "Frank" who scored for Spurs in both the Semi-Final Replay and the Final?

979.   Spurs beat this "City" 2-0 in the 5th Round. Name them.

980.   Who captained Spurs to victory?

LEGEND - DAVE MACKAY

981.   In which year did Bill Nicholson sign Dave - 1958, 1959 or
        1960?

982.   From which Scottish Club did Spurs sign him?

983.   To the nearest £5,000, how much did Dave cost Spurs?

984.   Name the player who Dave succeeded as Spurs captain during
        the mid-1960s.

985.   Which club did Dave join when he left White Hart Lane?

986.   Against which London club did Dave score a hat-trick in 1962?

987.   Can you recall the Manchester United player who Dave tackled
        in a 1962-1963 European Cup Winners' Cup tie, resulting in
        Dave breaking his left leg?

988.   In 1969 Dave shared the FWA Footballer of the Year award with
        a Manchester City defender. Name the City player.

989.   Which team did Dave manage to the First Division
        Championship title in 1975?

990.   In which oil-rich country did he coach from 1978 to 1987?

TRIVIA - 15

991. Can you name the only player to have played for Spurs who was the club captain for a Premier League winning side?

992. Can you name the goalkeeper who scored for Spurs in a Friendly against a Guernsey FA XI in 1985?

993. What former Spurs' legend once said: "His tackle was definitely pre-ordained."

994. Who played in all of Spurs' 58 competitive games in season 1970-1971 scoring 18 times?

995. What goalscoring feat was Spurs' 1920's legendary striker, Frank Osborne, the first and only Spurs player to achieve?

996. Name the Spurs player who was voted the PFA Player of the Year in 1994-95.

997. To the nearest 50, how many appearances did Pat Jennings make for Spurs including friendlies?

998. How many full international England caps did Paul Gascoigne win - 47, 57 or 67?

999. Can you name the "Andy" who played his last game for Spurs against Chelsea on 27 February 1994?

1000. What was the name of the song recorded by Glenn Hoddle and Chris Waddle during the 1980s?

LEGEND - DAVID GINOLA

1001.   Which club did David join in 1995?

1002.   In which year did David sign for Spurs?

1003.   What Paris-based club did David play for in season 1988-1989?

1004.   Can you name the future Premier League winning goalkeeper who David scored against when France beat England 2-0 at the 1987 Toulon Under-21 Tournament?

1005.   At which London club's ground did David win a "B" cap when England beat France 3-0 on 18 February 1992?

1006.   Against which London club did David score his first FA Cup goal?

1007.   Name either award that David won in season 1993-1994.

1008.   In which season did David win the PFA Player of the Year and Football Writers' Player of the Year awards?

1009.   Which club did David join when he left White Hart Lane?

1010.   Name the Red Cross Campaign for which David is an international spokesperson.

LEGEND - TEDDY SHERINGHAM

1011.   At which club did Teddy begin his Professional career?

1012.   Can you name the club Teddy joined in 1991?

1013.   In which year did Teddy first sign for Spurs?

1014.   To the nearest £250,000, how much did Spurs pay for Teddy in Q1013?

1015.   How many full England international caps did he win during his career - 50, 51 or 52?

1016.   In which year did Spurs sell Teddy to Manchester United?

1017.   Against which club did Teddy make his Manchester United debut?

1018.   Which club did Teddy sign for when he left White Hart Lane at the end of the 2002-2003 season?

1019.   Apart from the FA Premier League, FA Cup and UEFA Champions League, which other trophy did Teddy win with Manchester United in 1999?

1020.   Can you name the club which Teddy signed for in the summer of 2004?

LEGEND - ERIK THORSTVEDT

1021.   Can you recall the year in which Erik signed for Spurs?

1022.   Name the Spurs manager who brought Erik to White Hart Lane.

1023.   Against what oil-rich country did Erik make his full international debut for Norway?

1024.   In which 1984 international tournament did Erik represent Norway?

1025.   Which Bundesliga club did he sign for in 1985?

1026.   Can you recall the goalkeeper that Erik was bought to replace at Spurs?

1027.   What nickname was Erik known by during his playing career?

1028.   To whom did Erik lose his place in the Spurs team in 1994?

1029.   In how many full internationals did Erik play for Norway - 97, 98 or 99?

1030.   Name the club that Erik had agreed to join in 1995 but didn't as a result of failing a medical.

JERMAIN DEFOE

1031.   In which part of East London was Jermain born?

1032.   Which London club's Youth Team did Jermain progress through before leaving them in July 1999?

1033.   From which club did Spurs buy Jermain?

1034.   In which year did Jermain arrive at White Hart Lane?

1035.   Against which Scandinavian country did Jermain make his full international debut for England?

1036.   Can you recall the country who Jermain scored his first full international England goal against on 9 September 2004?

1037.   With which club was linked with a possible move prior to the closure of the transfer window in January 2005?

1038.   What is Jermain's 2004-2005 squad number at Spurs?

1039.   Can you recall the seaside club where Jermain spent 7 months on loan during the 2000-2001 season, scoring 19 goals in 31 appearances?

1040.   Name the Premier League club who Jermain made his debut for Spurs against, scoring in the game.

LEGEND - CHRIS HUGHTON

1041. What country did Chris adopt as a player?

1042. How many full international caps did Chris win - 53, 54 or 55?

1043. What occupation might Chris have taken up had he not made it as a Professional footballer - an accountant, a doctor or an engineer?

1044. To the nearest 25, how many League appearances did Chris make for Spurs?

1045. What was the first domestic trophy that Chris won with Spurs?

1046. Can you recall Chris's official position at Spurs in season 1999-2000?

1047. In which year did Chris play his last game for Spurs?

1048. Can you recall the opposition when Chris made his last appearance for the club?

1049. What was the last trophy that Chris won with Spurs?

1050. Apart from Martin Jol, to which other manager was Chris an assistant to in 2004-2005?

EXPERT - BILL NICHOLSON

1051.   To which team did Spurs send Bill to gain some playing experience with in 1936?

1052.   Can you recall the Lancashire team that Bill made his Spurs debut against?

1053.   Name any of the clubs that Bill played for during the Second World War.

1054.   Bill only won 1 full England cap during his career. Can you name the European side he won it against?

1055.   Who was Bill's manager at Spurs when they won the Second and First Division Championships in successive seasons?

1056.   Name either of the 2 men who Bill Nicholson recommended to the Spurs Board to replace him as manager in 1974-75.

1057.   Which Spurs manager brought Bill back to White Hart Lane in a consultancy role?

1058.   Name the club, managed by Ron Greenwood, of which Bill was made the chief scout almost 20 years after he left Spurs as a player.

1059.   After losing which Cup Final did Bill consider retiring as Spurs manager?

1060.   What was Bill's official role at Spurs up until his sad death on 23 October 2004?

EXPERT - HISTORY

1061. When the club was first formed it was named after the Duke of Northumberland's famous son. Can you name him?

1062. Where in Tottenham did the club play their first matches?

1063. Can you recall the name the club adopted in 1884?

1064. Against what "St" or in what "London Cup" did the club play their first competitive match in 1885?

1065. In 1888 Spurs moved home. At what "Park" did they now play their home games?

1066. What significant change occurred to the club's kit in 1898?

1067. To which League were Spurs elected in 1896?

1068. What significant "symbolic" change was made to one of the stands at White Hart Lane in 1909?

1069. Spurs won the FA Cup for the second time in 1921, but can you name the ground where the Final was played?

1070. Which Castle can be found on the club shield?

EXPERT - WINNERS

*ALL YOU HAVE TO DO HERE IS ASSOCIATE THE
COMPETITION WITH THE YEAR SPURS WON IT*

1071.	Southern District Charity Cup	1945
1072.	Sun International Challenge Trophy	1929
1073.	London League Premier Division	1920
1074.	Football League Division 2	1904
1075.	Football League South	1921
1076.	FA Charity Shield	1934
1077.	Dewar Shield	1907
1078.	FA Cup	1903
1079.	London Challenge Cup	1983
1080.	Western League	1952

EXPERT - LEGEND -
JURGEN KLINSMANN

1081.   At which German club did Jurgen begin his Professional career?

1082.   Can you name either of the 2 clubs he was at prior to joining the club in Q1081?

1083.   Name the German club he joined after he left the team in Q1081.

1084.   How many seasons did he spend at the team in Q1083?

1085.   In which year did he make his full international debut for Germany?

1086.   To the nearest 10, how many full international appearances did he make for Germany?

1087.   In which season was he the Bundesliga's top goalscorer with 19 goals?

1088.   Can you recall the year he was voted the German Footballer of the Year?

1089.   Which team did he join immediately after leaving Inter Milan?

1090.   What was the highest ever position reached by Jurgen in the voting for the FIFA World Player of the Year?

EXPERT - LEGEND -
STEVE PERRYMAN

1091.   How many League Cup Winners' tankards did Steve win?

1092.   Following on from Q1091, in which year did he win his last League Cup Winners' medal?

1093.   Which team gave Steve his first managerial job?

1094.   Can you recall the club who Steve became the manager of after he left the club in Q1093?

1095.   In between the jobs in Q1093 and Q1094, can you recall the North East club that Steve was scouting for?

1096.   Steve returned to White Hart Lane as Spurs' assistant manager. Can you recall who he was the assistant to when he arrived?

1097.   Can you recall the name of the Japanese team for which Steve took up the position of assistant manager, to the same man he was the assistant to at Spurs, in 1996?

1098.   Which club made Steve their Director of Football in 2003?

1099.   Can you recall the Cup Winners' Cup that Steve won as a manager?

1100.   Apart from the team in Q1097, which other J-League side did Steve manage?

EXPERT - SPURS v ARSENAL

1101. Up to the end of 2004, what is Spurs longest sequence of games without a win against Arsenal?

1102. What is the highest number of total career goals scored by a Spurs player against Arsenal?

1103. Following on from Q1102, can you name any of the players who hold this record?

1104. To the nearest 10, how many times did Spurs play Arsenal in the First Division?

1105. Following on from Q1104, and again to the nearest 10, how many times did Spurs beat Arsenal in the First Division?

1106. Name the Terry, whose surname sounds like a household appliance, and who was the last Spurs player to score a hat-trick against Arsenal.

1107. Up to the end of 2004, how many times has Spurs met Arsenal in the League Cup?

1108. Why was Spurs' Southern District Combination game against Arsenal abandoned after 75 minutes on 24 April 1900?

1109. Can you name the "Charity Fund" competition in which Spurs played Arsenal 3 times, winning all 3 games without conceding a goal?

1110. In which "War Cup" competition has Spurs played Arsenal twice, losing at home and winning away by the same score, 3-0?

EXPERT - TRIVIA - 1

1111. How many goals did Jimmy Greaves score for Spurs against Arsenal?

1112. In which "Chair" was Paul Gascoigne photographed drinking prior to Euro 1996?

1113. Up to the end of 2006, how many times has a Spurs player scored a hat-trick against Arsenal?

1114. In which country did Steve Perryman win his first Championship medal either as a player or a manager?

1115. In which year did Gary Lineker win the Spanish Cup with Barcelona?

1116. Name the English "City" who Spurs beat to win the Nolia Cup in Sweden in 1977.

1117. In which year was Jurgen Klinsmann appointed the captain of Germany?

1118. Can you name the Lancashire lower League side who put Spurs out of the 2002-2003 League Cup?

1119. Name the Chinese club that Paul Gascoigne played for in 2003.

1120. Which club did Spurs pay a then club record transfer fee of £1.5 million for Paul Stewart to?

EXPERT - SPURS v CHELSEA

1121. Who is the last man to have played for both Spurs and Chelsea and also to have managed the 2 clubs?

1122. Name either of the 2 players involved in a swap deal between the 2 clubs in December 1959.

1123. Who left Chelsea to join Spurs in a £700,000 transfer deal in June 1992?

1124. To the nearest £100,000, how much was the biggest transfer deal involving 1 player leaving his club for the other?

1125. Can you name the Spurs striker from the 1980s who spent a period on loan at Chelsea?

1126. Who made a scoring debut for Spurs against Chelsea on 5 December 1992?

1127. On 3 April 1973, 4 of the Spurs players who played Chelsea had surnames beginning with the letter "P". Can you recall any 3 of the 4?

1128. 2 players made their Spurs debut against Chelsea on 13 September 2003. Name either of the 2.

1129. Name the "Alex" who scored on his debut for Spurs against Chelsea on 3 March 1951, which proved to be his first and last goal for the club.

1130. Which "Allen" played his last game for Spurs against Chelsea on 19 December 1998?

EXPERT - LEGEND -
JIMMY GREAVES

1131.   Which major trophy did Jimmy win with Spurs in 1963?

1132.   Against which team did Jimmy once score 4 goals in a 9-2 win for Spurs?

1133.   How many League goals did Jimmy score from 41 games in season 1963-1964?

1134.   Can you recall Jimmy's new striking partner who arrived at the club in December 1964?

1135.   What illness struck Jimmy in October 1965, which looked certain to ruin his chances of making England's 1966 World Cup squad?

1136.   Can you name the player who replaced an injured Jimmy for England's 1966 World Cup Quarter-Final match?

1137.   Spurs finished 3rd in the First Division in 1967, but what trophy did Jimmy help them win?

1138.   How many goals did Jimmy score for England in full internationals?

1139.   Can you name the club who Jimmy joined after he left Spurs?

1140.   Following on from Q1139, which player came to Spurs in the same deal?

EXPERT - CUP FINALS

1141.   Who was the Spurs player/manager in the 1901 FA Cup Final?

1142.   Name any 1 of the 4 "Jimmys" who played for Spurs in the 1921 FA Cup Final.

1143.   Who was the Spurs goalkeeper in the 1961 FA Cup Final?

1144.   How many major Cups did Spurs win under Bill Nicholson's management?

1145.   Which four managers have led Spurs to a League Cup Final?

1146.   Can you name the Spurs player who came on as a substitute, much to the fans' delight, for Paul Miller in the 1984 UEFA Cup Final 2nd Leg?

1147.   What was the penalty shoot-out score in the 1984 UEFA Cup Final?

1148.   Following on from Q1147, can you name a Spurs player who missed from the spot?

1149.   Who is the only Spurs player to score in both an League Cup Final and a UEFA Cup Final for the club?

1150.   Name the player who played for Spurs in the 1962 FA Cup Final but was an unused substitute in the 1967 Final.

EXPERT - TERRY VENABLES

1151.   How many Cup games in total did Spurs play under Terry
          from 1987-1991?

1152.   Can you recall how many Cup games Spurs lost under Terry
          from 1987-1991?

1153.   Spurs recorded 6 consecutive wins under Terry from 21 March
          1990 to 21 April 1990. Name the player who scored in the first
          4 of these games.

1154.   Which London club beat Spurs 2-1 on the opening day of the
          1989-1990 season?

1155.   In season 1990-1991 Spurs went 14 League games unbeaten.
          Can you name the Lancashire club who brought the run to an
          end?

1156.   Which team did Spurs play twice in the last 4 games of the
          1990-1991 season?

1157.   In the 1990-91 League Cup, 2 Spurs players scored in Rounds
          2, 3 and 4. Name either of them.

1158.   Which country were England's first opponents with Terry
          Venables as their manager?

1159.   Can you recall England's last opponents with Terry Venables as
          their manager?

1160.   Name the Spurs player who scored his first goal for England
          under Terry Venables against Greece at Wembley on 12 May
          1994.

EXPERT - TRIVIA - 2

1161.	Clive Allen scored a hat-trick for Spurs on the opening day of the 1986-1987 season, but can you name the Southampton and Northern Ireland striker who was the first Division 1 player to score a hat-trick that season, beating Clive to it by 10 minutes?

1162.	What award did Frank Arnesen win in 1979?

1163.	Name the Spurs striker who played his last game for the club against Leicester City in April 1985.

1164.	Only 2 players have scored for Spurs in both an FA Cup Final and a European Cup Winners' Cup Final. Name either of them.

1165.	How many League goals did Spurs score in season 1978-1979?

1166.	Can you name the future Spurs player who scored for his country in the 1986 World Cup 3rd/4th Place Play-Off match?

1167.	Who scored in all of Spurs' 1986-1987 League Cup ties until they were eliminated in the Semi-Final Replay?

1168.	Why was Jimmy Greaves not permitted to play for Spurs for 3 weeks after he signed for them from AC Milan?

1169.	Name the former legend who played for Barnet, Brentwood Town, Chelmsford City and Woodford Town after he left Spurs.

1170.	Up to the 2004-2005 season, who was the last player to score a penalty for Spurs in a European tie?

EXPERT - LEGEND - GARY MABBUTT

1171. When Gary's contract at Spurs ended in 1987 can you name either the French side or the Spanish side that were interested in signing him?

1172. Under how many different managers did Gary play at Spurs?

1173. Who was the Spurs manager when he joined Spurs?

1174. What age was Gary when he retired from playing professional football?

1175. How many FA Cup Finals did he appear in for Spurs?

1176. In which year did he score a goal in the FA Cup Final?

1177. In which year did Gary sign for Spurs?

1178. To the nearest £10,000, how much did he cost Spurs?

1179. What was Gary awarded in January 1994?

1180. Name either the country that Gary made his full international England debut against or the country he scored his only England goal against.

EXPERT - LEGEND - MARTIN CHIVERS

1181. Where in England was Martin born?

1182. To the nearest £10,000, how much did Martin cost Spurs?

1183. When was Martin's last season at White Hart Lane?

1184. Against which "United" did he score his last goal for Spurs?

1185. To the nearest 50, how many competitive games did Martin play for Spurs?

1186. Name the 2 managers that Martin played under at Spurs.

1187. In which season did Martin score 33 times for Spurs in 61 appearances?

1188. Which Norwegian side did Martin score 5 times against in the 1972-73 UEFA Cup?

1189. To the nearest 20, how many goals did Martin score for Spurs?

1190. Against which "United" did he make his last appearance for Spurs?

EXPERT -
SPURS v WEST HAM UNITED

1191.   To the nearest 5,000, what is Spurs' biggest home attendance against West Ham United?

1192.   To the nearest 5,000, what is West Ham United's biggest home attendance against Spurs?

1193.   What is Spurs' biggest home defeat to West Ham United?

1194.   What is Spurs' biggest away defeat to West Ham United?

1195.   What is the highest aggregate of goals in a match between Spurs and West Ham United?

1196.   Name the Spurs player who joined West Ham United as part of the £4 million deal that brought Frederic Kanoute to White Hart Lane in August 2003?

1197.   Who joined West Ham United from Spurs in January 2003?

1198.   Can you name the "Paul" who joined Spurs from West Ham United in June 1985?

1199.   What was significant about Spurs' League Cup tie against West Ham United on 14 September 1966?

1200.   Name the player who made the 400th League appearance of his career against West Ham United on 14 January 1995.

EXPERT - LEGEND - GLENN HODDLE

1201. In which year was Glenn appointed the player/manager of Swindon Town?

1202. Can you recall the year he was appointed the manager of Chelsea?

1203. Who succeeded Glenn as England manager in a caretaker capacity?

1204. Name the manager he replaced at Spurs.

1205. Name the faith healer who Glenn used prior to him being sacked as England Manager.

1206. Of which club was he appointed manager in 2000?

1207. Can you name the former Spurs Legend who first spotted Glenn playing in a Junior Cup Final before suggesting that Spurs should sign him?

1208. Who was the Spurs manager when Glenn made his debut for the club?

1209. What was Glenn's only success as a manager?

1210. Can you recall the name of the book he released after the 1998 World Cup Finals?

EXPERT - TRIVIA - 3

1211.   Name the Spurs player who played in all 58 competitive games for the club in 1970-1971, scoring 34 times.

1212.   Against which "United" did Spurs record their biggest win, 4-1, during 1995-1996?

1213.   Name the recent signing who scored on his debut for Spurs at the start of the 1978-1979 season.

1214.   Can you name the player who Spurs paid a British record fee of £200,000 for in 1970?

1215.   How many goals did Clive Allen score in all competitions for Spurs in season 1986-1987?

1216.   Against which London club was Ossie Ardiles's last match as Spurs manager?

1217.   To the nearest 5, how many career goals did Steve Perryman score for Spurs?

1218.   How many times has Spurs reached the Semi-Final stage in the three major European competitions?

1219.   To the nearest 5, how many goals did Jurgen Klinsmann score for Germany in full internationals?

1220.   Name the player who scored 21 League goals for Spurs in season 1983-1984.

LEGEND - JOHN PRATT

1221. In which year did John sign as a Professional for Spurs - 1965, 1966 or 1967?

1222. Against which London club did John make his debut for Spurs?

1223. Can you recall the "wood-sounding" team that John joined in the USA after he left White Hart Lane?

1224. To which Spurs manager was John the Spurs assistant for a brief while during the mid-1980s?

1225. John's last match was a 4-1 defeat against Manchester United away on 12 May 1980. Can you name the former Spurs legend whose last match for the club was also in a 4-1 loss to Manchester United at Old Trafford?

1226. To the nearest 50, how many total appearances did John make for Spurs?

1227. To the nearest 5, how many total goals did John score for Spurs?

1228. Against what "City" did John score 5 goals during his career at White Hart Lane, the most he's scored against any club?

1229. What was the first trophy that John won with Spurs?

1230. In October and November 1972 John scored goals against two England goalkeepers. Name them both.

LEGEND - JOHN WHITE

1231.   From which Scottish club did Spurs sign John?

1232.   What was John's occupation whilst he was playing football in Scotland before Bill Nicholson signed him?

1233.   In what "running" sport did John excel prior to signing for Spurs?

1234.   To the nearest £2,000, how much did he cost Spurs?

1235.   In which year did John sign for Spurs - 1958, 1959 or 1960?

1236.   What was John's nickname at White Hart Lane?

1237.   Can you recall the first trophy that John won with Spurs?

1238.   To the nearest 50, how many League appearances did John make for Spurs?

1239.   To the nearest 5, how many total goals did John score for Spurs?

1240.   How did John sadly die on 21 July 1964?

LEGEND - DARREN ANDERTON

1241. In which year did Darren join Spurs?

1242. From which club did he join Spurs?

1243. To the nearest £250,000, how much did he cost Spurs?

1244. How many full international England caps did Darren win - 29, 30 or 31?

1245. Can you recall how many goals he scored for England?

1246. Against what south coast club did he score his first Spurs Premier League goal?

1247. What was Darren's "unfortunate" nickname at the club?

1248. In which competition did Darren score his first goal for Spurs?

1249. To the nearest 25, how many total appearances did Darren make for Spurs?

1250. To the nearest 5, how many total goals did Darren score for Spurs?

ANSWERS

BILL NICHOLSON

1.　　Scarborough (26 January 1919)
2.　　1938
3.　　Left back
4.　　1
5.　　He scored
6.　　Cambridge University
7.　　England (at the 1958 World Cup Finals)
8.　　1958
9.　　1974-1975
10.　　Terry Neill

SEASON 2004-2005

11.　　Liverpool
12.　　1-1
13.　　Newcastle United (1-0 away on 21 August)
14.　　Jermain Defoe
15.　　The Team Coach
16.　　Oldham Athletic
17.　　Manchester United (at White Hart Lane on 25 September)
18.　　Bolton Wanderers (in the Premier League & Carling Cup respectively)
19.　　Crystal Palace (28 December)
20.　　Everton (5-2 at White Hart Lane on New Year's Day)

ROBBIE KEANE

21.　　Czech Republic
22.　　Wolverhampton Wanderers
23.　　Coventry City
24.　　Inter Milan
25.　　Leeds United
26.　　2002 (30 August)
27.　　West Ham United (at White Hart Lane on 14 September 2002)
28.　　5
29.　　Everton
30.　　Niall Quinn

THE DOUBLE

31.　　1960-61
32.　　15
33.　　Everton
34.　　11
35.　　Sheffield Wednesday (2-1 away on 2 November 1960)
36.　　Aston Villa (Villa Park)
37.　　Charlton Athletic (3-2 at home on 7 January 1961)
38.　　115
39.　　Leicester City

40.   16 (1 more than they won at home)

LEGEND - DANNY BLANCHFLOWER
41.   Belfast (10 February 1926)
42.   Glentoran
43.   Barnsley
44.   Aston Villa
45.   Scotland (at Windsor Park, Belfast on 1 October 1949)
46.   1958 (Sweden)
47.   Arsenal
48.   £30,000
49.   The European Cup Winners' Cup
50.   Chelsea

LEGEND - GARY LINEKER
51.   Leicester (30 November 1960)
52.   Leicester City
53.   Everton
54.   Barcelona
55.   1984
56.   Scotland
57.   48
58.   The Second Division Championship with Leicester City in 1980
59.   The FA Cup (1991)
60.   Arsene Wenger

KEITH BURKINSHAW
61.   1975
62.   First Team coach
63.   Terry Neill
64.   1976
65.   Ipswich Town (lost 3-1 away on 21 August 1976)
66.   Scunthorpe
67.   They were relegated to Division 2
68.   4th (on 2 occasions)
69.   FA Cup (1981)
70.   1983-84

UEFA CUP WINNERS - 1984
71.   Keith Burkinshaw
72.   Anderlecht
73.   1-1
74.   1-1
75.   Paul Miller (1st Leg) & Graham Roberts (2nd Leg)
76.   Drogheda United
77.   Hajduk Split
78.   Bayern Munich
79.   Austria Vienna
80.   Hadjuk Split (lost 2-1 away and won 1-0 at home)

HISTORY
81.   1882
82.   Hotspur Football Club

83.   Cricket (Hotspur Cricket Club)
84.   Arsenal (or Royal Arsenal as they were known then)
85.   Red shirts & navy shorts
86.   Notts County (1899)
87.   They became the only non-League club to win the FA Cup
88.   Wolverhampton Wanderers (Spurs won 3-0)
89.   The Second Division Championship
90.   To Dare Is To Do

IT HAPPENED THIS YEAR
91.   Spurs appear in 8th FA Cup Final   1987
92.   Kit is changed to white shirts and shorts   1985
93.   UEFA Cup winners   1972
94.   Spurs sign their first "£1 million plus" player   1988
95.   Club Shield introduced   1957
96.   New West Stand opened   1982
97.   Promotion to Division 1   1978
98.   Spurs first played in European competition   1961
99.   League Cup winners   1973
100.   Record attendance for White Hart Lane set   1938

WINNERS
101.   Anglo-Italian League Cup   1971
102.   European Cup Winners' Cup   1963
103.   Football League Cup   1999
104.   Football League Division 1   1951
105.   Football League Division 2   1950
106.   FA Charity Shield (joint winners)   1967
107.   Dewar Shield   1902
108.   FA Cup   1921
109.   London Challenge Cup   1910
110.   Southern League   1900

TRIVIA - 1
111.   Paul Stewart
112.   Float shares on the London Stock Exchange
113.   The Shelf
114.   Chris Armstrong
115.   Keith Burkinshaw
116.   1986 & 1992
117.   The FA Cup (1901)
118.   Steve Perryman
119.   Pat Jennings
120.   Manchester United (3-2 on penalties)

DIMITAR BERBATOV
121.   2006
122.   Bayer Leverkusen
123.   £10.9m
124.   Reading (in a 6-4 Premier League win)
125.   CSKA Sofia
126.   Manchester United

127.	1999
128.	39 (in 61 appearances for Bulgaria)
129.	Bolton Wanderers (on 19th August 2006)
130.	Sheffield United (on 22nd August 2006 at White Hart Lane)

THE MANAGERS

131.	Peter Shreeves	1984-1986
132.	Ossie Ardiles	1993-1994
133.	George Graham	1998-2001
134.	David Pleat	1986-1987
135.	Keith Burkinshaw	1976-1984
136.	Peter Shreeves	1991-1992
137.	Terry Venables	1987-1991
138.	Gerry Francis	1994-1997
139.	Christian Gross	1997-1998
140.	Glenn Hoddle	2001-2003

LEGEND - JURGEN KLINSMANN

141.	1994
142.	Monaco
143.	Ilie Dumitrescu & Gica Popescu
144.	Ossie Ardiles
145.	1 (1994-95)
146.	Bayern Munich
147.	UEFA Cup
148.	Inter Milan
149.	Sampdoria
150.	1990 (in Italy)

HAT-TRICKS

151.	Jurgen Klinsmann	Wimbledon - 2 May 1998
152.	Jermain Defoe	Southampton - 18 December 2004
153.	Gordon Durie	Coventry City - 28 March 1992
154.	Frederic Kanoute	Crystal Palace - 3 January 2004
155.	Robbie Keane	Everton - 12 January 2003
156.	Teddy Sheringham	Hereford United - 17 January 1996
157.	Gary Lineker	QPR - 30 September 1989
158.	Les Ferdinand	Bolton - 11 December 2001
159.	Paul Gascoigne	Derby County - 8 September 1990
160.	Steffen Iversen	Southampton - 11 March 2000

SEASON 2003-2004

161.	Birmingham City
162.	13
163.	Crystal Palace (3-0 at White Hart Lane)
164.	Mauricio Taricco & Frederic Kanoute
165.	Coventry City
166.	Robbie Keane (in a 2-0 away win at Wolves)
167.	Orlando Pirates (lost 2-1) & Kaiser Chiefs (won 2-0)
168.	Bobby Zamora (v West Ham United)
169.	Middlesbrough
170.	Manchester City

TRIVIA - 2

171.	1986
172.	Jurgen Klinsmann
173.	Keith Burkinshaw
174.	7th
175.	1994-95
176.	Robbie Keane (against Wolves, Spurs won 5-2)
177.	Standard Liege (1-0)
178.	Les Ferdinand
179.	Jurgen Klinsmann
180.	14th

LEGEND - CLIFF JONES

181.	1958
182.	Hockey & rugby
183.	Swansea Town (now Swansea City)
184.	On the wing
185.	19
186.	The first non-playing substitute in an FA Cup Final
187.	1968
188.	Fulham
189.	A broken leg
190.	176

SEASON 2005-2006

191.	Jermain Defoe
192.	FC Porto
193.	Leicester City
194.	Chelsea (2-0 at White Hart Lane on 27th August)
195.	Ledley King
196.	Grimsby Town
197.	The Peace Cup
198.	Jermain Defoe, Robbie Keane & Mido
199.	Michael Carrick
200.	West Ham United

SEASON 2006-07 - 1

201.	5th
202.	Sheffield United (2-0 on 22nd August 2006 at White Hart Lane)
203.	17
204.	Aston Villa
205.	Watford
206.	Portsmouth
207.	Inter Milan
208.	Cardiff City
209.	60 (W17, D9, L12)
210.	Pascal Chimbonda

LEGEND - PAUL GASCOIGNE - 1

211.	Newcastle United
212.	4
213.	112

214.	1988
215.	SS Lazio
216.	Terry Venables
217.	1990 (Italy)
218.	Glasgow Rangers
219.	Middlesbrough & Everton
220.	Burnley

LEDLEY KING
221.	1998-99 (as a sub on 1st May)
222.	Liverpool (3-2 away defeat)
223.	18
224.	Deadley Ledley, Ledders, Super Leds
225.	No.26
226.	1997
227.	The fastest goal in the FA Premier League (10 seconds v Bradford City in December 2000, his first for the club)
228.	2000
229.	Peter Taylor (when he was the Caretaker Manager)
230.	Antiguan

TRIVIA - 3
231.	1996
232.	Manchester City
233.	December 2004
234.	15th
235.	1993-94
236.	Terry Venables
237.	Sunderland
238.	80
239.	The 1984 UEFA Cup Final (2nd Leg at White Hart Lane on 25 May 1984)
240.	Dundee United

SPURS v ARSENAL - 1
241.	Sol Campbell (2001)
242.	Chris McGrath
243.	Pat van den Hauwe
244.	Neil Ruddock
245.	John Pratt
246.	Nourredine Naybet
247.	Gica Popescu
248.	It was Glenn Hoddle's first match in charge of Spurs
249.	Cyril Knowles
250.	Jermain Defoe

SPURS v CHELSEA
251.	Neil Sullivan (August 2003)
252.	Micky Hazard
253.	Gordon Durie
254.	Kerry Dixon
255.	Glenn Hoddle was the player/manager of Chelsea
256.	Alfie Conn
257.	Jack Taylor (he was the referee in charge of the 1974 World Cup Final)

258.	Neil McNab
259.	Steve Sedgley
260.	Gustavo Poyet (June 2001)

LEGEND - STEVE PERRYMAN

261.	Spurs (in July 1967)
262.	1969 (against Sunderland in September)
263.	The League Cup (1971)
264.	1981
265.	30 (v Iceland)
266.	The Football Writers' Association Footballer of the Year Award
267.	1985-86
268.	The UEFA Cup
269.	Oxford United
270.	MBE

TRIVIA - 4

271.	Steve Perryman
272.	Colin Calderwood
273.	Sol Campbell
274.	OBE
275.	Danny Blanchflower
276.	Alfie Conn (1974)
277.	He became the first substitute used by Spurs in a League match
278.	Keith Burkinshaw
279.	16 (on 3 occasions)
280.	1992-93, 1994-95 & 1995-96

SEASON 2001-2002

281.	Aston Villa
282.	14
283.	Coventry City
284.	Christian Ziege
285.	Fulham & Chelsea
286.	Manchester United
287.	Les Ferdinand, Dean Richards & Christian Ziege
288.	Chelsea (4-0 loss at White Hart Lane in Round 6)
289.	Bolton Wanderers & Tranmere Rovers
290.	Bill Nicholson (Spurs beat Fiorentina 3-0)

LEGEND - PAUL GASCOIGNE - 2

291.	Kevin Keegan
292.	Middlesbrough
293.	SS Lazio
294.	107
295.	Glasgow Rangers (v Hibernian)
296.	Jack Charlton
297.	Norway
298.	33
299.	Colin Hendry
300.	Teddy Sheringham

SPURS v ARSENAL - 2

301.   Clive Allen (2 League Cup Semi-Finals & League Cup Semi-Final Replay)
302.   Spurs 4 Arsenal 5
303.   1999-2000 (Spurs 2, Arsenal 1)
304.   Steffen Iversen & Tim Sherwood
305.   Gary Doherty (2001 Semi-Final at Old Trafford, Spurs lost 2-1)
306.   Robbie Keane
307.   Paul Stewart (1-1 at White Hart Lane on 22 February 1992)
308.   1991 (0-0 at Wembley)
309.   Gary Lineker
310.   (Spurs 1, Arsenal 0 - White Hart Lane on 12 December 1992)

SPURS IN THE FA CUP - 1

311.   Coventry City (1987)
312.   Sheffield United
313.   8
314.   True (5-3)
315.   1 (1987 loss to Coventry City)
316.   Nottingham Forest (1991)
317.   3 (1901, 1981 & 1982)
318.   Nottingham Forest (5th Round Replay)
319.   Gary Mabbutt (1991)
320.   Sheffield United (1901), Queen's Park Rangers (1981) & Manchester City (1982)

LEGEND - PAT JENNINGS

321.   Newry Town
322.   Watford
323.   Bill Nicholson
324.   £27,000
325.   The FA Cup (1967)
326.   1964
327.   Manchester United (at Old Trafford in a 3-3 draw on 12 August 1967)
328.   The PFA Player of the Year Award
329.   The League Cup (1973)
330.   Arsenal (1977)

TRIVIA - 5

331.   Danny Blanchflower (1961 & 1962) & Steve Perryman (1981 & 1982)
332.   Pat Jennings (Northern Ireland)
333.   The FA Cup (1894)
334.   Manchester United (11) & Arsenal (10)
335.   Alan Mullery
336.   Boston United (Howard Wilkinson was their player/manager and
        Paul Gascoigne played for them)
337.   1982
338.   Benfica (2-1)
339.   VfB Stuttgart
340.   5

FA CUP WINNERS - 1961

341.   Crewe Alexandra
342.   Aston Villa (Aston Villa away in Round 5 and the Semi-Final at Villa Park)
343.   Sunderland

344.	1 (Sunderland in Round 6)
345.	Les Allen
346.	Danny Blanchflower
347.	5-0 (against Sunderland in their Round 6 Replay)
348.	Bobby Smith
349.	2
350.	Spurs 2, Leicester City 0

SEASON 2000-2001

351.	Ipswich Town
352.	13
353.	Leyton Orient
354.	Manchester City (1-0 on 10 February 2001)
355.	Sergei Rebrov
356.	Newcastle United
357.	Birmingham City (3-1 at White Hart Lane in Round 3)
358.	Arsenal (in the Semi-Final)
359.	Manchester United
360.	Willem Korsten

LEGEND - RAY CLEMENCE

361.	Scunthorpe
362.	Liverpool
363.	Bill Shankly
364.	£300,000
365.	1981
366.	FA Cup (1982)
367.	5 (1972/73, 1975/76, 1976/77, 1978/79 & 1979/80)
368.	330
369.	3
370.	Middlesbrough (in a 3-1 away win on 29 August 1981)

UEFA CUP WINNERS - 1972

371.	Wolverhampton Wanderers
372.	Spurs won 2-1 away and drew 1-1 at home
373.	Martin Chivers (both goals in Spurs' 2-1 away win)
374.	Alan Mullery (in the 1-1 home draw)
375.	12
376.	Martin Chivers & Alan Gilzean
377.	Nantes
378.	Rapid Bucharest
379.	AC Milan
380.	Steve Perryman

EUROPEAN CUP WINNERS' CUP WINNERS - 1963

381.	Atletico Madrid
382.	Spurs 5, Atletico Madrid 1
383.	Terry Dyson & Jimmy Greaves
384.	Rotterdam
385.	7
386.	Glasgow Rangers
387.	Slovan Bratislava

388.	Shearer (Alan Shearer of Blackburn Rovers)
389.	1 (lost 2-0 to Slovan Bratislava in the 1st Leg of the Quarter-Final)
390.	John White

TRIVIA - 6

391.	Jurgen Klinsmann
392.	Ray Clemence
393.	Martin Peters (v Nantes)
394.	Japan's J-League Manager of the Year Award
395.	1992
396.	Alan Mullery
397.	7
398.	Douglas Alexiou
399.	Alf Ramsey
400.	Feyenoord

SPURS IN THE EUROPEAN CUP

401.	1961-1962
402.	Semi-Final
403.	Gornik Zabrze
404.	8
405.	Feyenoord
406.	Benfica
407.	Danny Blanchflower (he scored 2)
408.	Bobby Smith (6 goals)
409.	8 (against Gornik Zabrze in the 2nd Leg Preliminary Round)
410.	Dukla Prague

SPURS IN EUROPE

411.	Spurs also won the League Championship and so opted to play in the European Cup
412.	OFK Belgrade
413.	Bobby Smith
414.	Glasgow Rangers (Round 2, 1962-63 European Cup Winners' Cup)
415.	Poland (Gornik Zabrze)
416.	1999-2000
417.	The UEFA Cup
418.	The Intertoto Cup
419.	IFC Kaiserslautern
420.	IFC Cologne

SPURS IN THE UEFA CUP

421.	Graham Roberts
422.	Dimitar Berbatov
423.	Olympiakos Piraeus (1972-1973)
424.	Bayer Leverkusen, Besiktas, Club Bruges and Dinamo Bucharest
425.	FC Bruges
426.	Mark Falco (6 goals)
427.	Slavia Prague
428.	Czechoslovakia (Bohemians Prague)
429.	Martin Chivers
430.	Liverpool (Semi-Final, Spurs won 2-1 at home and lost 1-0 away)

SPURS IN THE EUROPEAN CUP WINNERS' CUP

431.   Manchester United (Round 2, 1963-64 European Cup Winners' Cup)
432.   Slovan Bratislava (1962-1963)
433.   FC Porto
434.   Terry Venables
435.   Terry Dyson, Jimmy Greaves & Dave Mackay
436.   Feyenoord (1991-1992 Quarter-Finals)
437.   Manchester United (Round 2, Spurs won 2-0 at home and lost 4-1 away)
438.   Jimmy Robertson
439.   1 - Coleraine (1982-1983 European Cup Winners' Cup)
440.   Gordon Durie (1) & Gary Lineker (2) (against FC Porto on 23 October 1991)

SPURS IN THE FA CUP - 2

441.   Crystal Palace
442.   Burnden Park (the former home of Bolton Wanderers)
443.   Terry Venables (1991)
444.   Paul Stewart & a Des Walker own goal
445.   Danny Blanchflower (1962)
446.   Glenn Hoddle
447.   Garth Crooks
448.   Milija Aleksic
449.   Manchester City
450.   Tommy Hutchinson (Manchester City)

LEAGUE CUP WINNERS - 1999

451.   Manchester United
452.   It was the only competition entered by Manchester United in season
        1998/1999 that they did not win (1999 Treble Winners)
453.   Leicester City
454.   Allan Nielsen
455.   Stephen Carr & Ramon Vega
456.   George Graham
457.   Chris Armstrong, Espen Baardsen, Jose Dominquez & Luke Young
458.   Ian Walker
459.   Wimbledon
460.   Chris Armstrong

LEGEND - GRAHAM ROBERTS

461.   Southampton
462.   West Bromwich Albion
463.   Weymouth
464.   Paul Miller
465.   1980
466.   The FA Cup (1981)
467.   The UEFA Cup Final (1984)
468.   Steve Hodge
469.   Keith Burkinshaw, David Pleat & Peter Shreeves
470.   Glasgow Rangers

TRIVIA - 7

471.   Liverpool (at White Hart Lane on 1 December)
472.   Leicester City

473.   He was suspended
474.   Ray Clemence (with Liverpool in 1977, 1978 & 1981)
475.   IFC Cologne, Luzern, Osters IF & Rudar Velenje
476.   Steffen Iversen (v IFC Kaiserslautern in the 1999-2000 UEFA Cup)
477.   67
478.   1951
479.   Terry Venables
480.   Feyenoord (1973-1974 UEFA Cup & 1991-92 European Cup Winners' Cup)

SPURS HEROES - 1
481.   He scored it against Southampton who rejected him
482.   Andy Sinton (for David Ginola)
483.   Teddy Sheringham (with Manchester United in 1999)
484.   Alan Mullery
485.   Ray Clemence
486.   Shimizu S-Pulse (in the J-League)
487.   105
488.   1982 (Spain)
489.   Brazil (December 1987 in a 1-1 draw)
490.   Boston United

OPPONENTS - 1
491.   Air raid on London (Arsenal were winning 3-2 at the time and the result stood)
492.   Liverpool
493.   Stevenage
494.   Wolverhampton Wanderers
495.   Bobby Smith
496.   Once
497.   6-0 (against Drogheda United in the 1st Round of the 1983-1984 UEFA Cup)
498.   Jimmy Greaves (he was at Chelsea at the time)
499.   Feyenoord
500.   Aberdeen (1973-1974 UEFA Cup) & Glasgow Rangers (1962-1963 European
         Cup Winners' Cup)

DAVID PLEAT
501.   Luton Town
502.   Shrewsbury Town
503.   Luton Town
504.   Exeter City, Peterborough United & Nuneaton (player/manager)
505.   Second Division Championship
506.   1986
507.   1987
508.   Olympiakos
509.   Leicester City
510.   Director of Football

LEGEND - OSSIE ARDILES
511.   1978 (in Argentina)
512.   FA Cup in 1981
513.   To prepare for the 1982 World Cup Finals
514.   Paris Saint-Germain
515.   The FA Cup Semi-Final 2-0 win over Leicester City
516.   Swindon Town

517.   West Bromwich Albion
518.   1993 (June)
519.   Notts County
520.   1994 (October)

LEGEND - JIMMY GREAVES
521.   West Ham United
522.   Chelsea
523.   Spurs
524.   AC Milan
525.   1961 (November)
526.   Blackpool
527.   21
528.   The FA Cup (1962)
529.   37
530.   Ted Harper (1930-1931) & Bobby Smith (1957-1958)

TRIVIA - 8
531.   Ossie's Dream
532.   Chas 'N' Dave
533.   3
534.   Terry Venables & Glenn Hoddle
535.   Jimmy Greaves (for Chelsea)
536.   1986 (Mexico)
537.   Giovanni Trapattoni
538.   Darren Anderton
539.   The UEFA Cup Final (1984)
540.   The European Cup Winners' Cup (1963)

LEGEND - CLIVE ALLEN
541.   Queen's Park Rangers
542.   1984 (August)
543.   Aston Villa
544.   16
545.   West Ham United
546.   33
547.   1987
548.   11
549.   1988
550.   Bordeaux

SEASON 2006-07 - 2
551.   Ben Foster (Watford)
552.   Arsenal (in the semi-finals)
553.   Steed Malbranque (in a 1-1 draw away to Portsmouth)
554.   Southend United, Spurs won 3-1
555.   104 (57 PL, 15 FA Cup, 12 LC & 20 Uefa Cup)
556.   Dimitar Berbatov & Robbie Keane
557.   Bordeaux & Nice
558.   Manchester City
559.   Newcastle United (on 14/1/2007, Manchester United won 4-0 on 4/2/2007)
560.   Chelsea (2-1 at White Hart Lane in a Replay)

SPURS v ARSENAL - THE FACTS

561.   5-0 (4 November 1901, 25 December 1911 & 4 April 1983)
562.   3-0 (4 times)
563.   6-0 (6 March 1935)
564.   5-0 (28 April 1906)
565.   9 (Spurs 4, Arsenal 5 - 13 November 2004 at White Hart Lane)
566.   69,821 (10 October 1953)
567.   72,164 (29 September 1951)
568.   1991 FA Cup Semi-Final at Wembley - 77,893
569.   4 (11 April 1977 - 26 December 1979)
570.   6 (18 December 1943 - 16 February 1946)

TRIVIA - 9

571.   Ossie Ardiles, Ricky Villa and Mario Kempes (who played for Spurs as a
          trialist in 1984)
572.   Inter Milan (1 May 1986)
573.   Liam Brady
574.   Joe Kinnear
575.   Nico Claesen
576.   Alan Shearer (1-1 v Germany in the Euro'96 Semi-Final at Wembley)
577.   Christian Ziege
578.   Spurs' previous game was against the same club, beating them 1-0 in the
          1999 Worthington (League) Cup Final
579.   Chris Armstrong (v Everton in a 4-1 home win)
580.   Arsenal Stadium (Highbury)

SPURS HEROES - 2

581.   Martin Peters (1966), Ossie Ardiles (1978), Jurgen Klinsmann (1990) &
          Christian Ziege (2002)
582.   Terry Yorath
583.   Gerry Armstrong
584.   Chris Armstrong
585.   Colin Calderwood
586.   Darren Anderton
587.   Steve Archibald (v New Zealand)
588.   Glenn Hoddle
589.   Garth Crooks
590.   Jimmy Greaves

OPPONENTS - 2

591.   Nottingham Forest
592.   England XI
593.   Wimbledon (Premier League 2, FA Cup 2 & Worthington Cup 2)
594.   Everton
595.   Arsenal (at Arsenal in the Premier League on 14 November)
596.   Manchester City (1981)
597.   Aston Villa
598.   Watford
599.   Norwich City
600.   Wolves

MARTIN JOL

601.   Den Haag (16 January 1956)

602.	Den Haag
603.	Dutch Player of the Year
604.	West Bromwich Albion
605.	Coventry City
606.	Tony Soprano
607.	Dutch Football Writers' Coach of the Year
608.	Jacques Santini
609.	Ajax Amsterdam
610.	Manchester United

EDGAR DAVIDS

611.	Surinam (in Paramaribo)
612.	Ajax Amsterdam
613.	Martin Jol (on 3rd August 2005)
614.	Inter Milan
615.	Free transfer
616.	Middlesbrough (2-0 home win on 20th August 2005)
617.	Juventus
618.	The Netherlands
619.	FC Barcelona
620.	1

STRANGE BUT TRUE

621.	Graeme Souness
622.	He was the first black player to play for the club (1909-1911)
623.	At Feyenoord's stadium (Spurs won the European Cup Winners' Cup there in 1963 and lost there to Feyenoord over 2 Legs in the 1973-74 UEFA Cup Final)
624.	Peter Taylor (he managed Leicester City)
625.	Brian Clough
626.	It was the first ever televised English League game (Spurs won 2-1)
627.	Terry Gibson
628.	Steve Archibald
629.	John Chiedozie
630.	David Pleat

PAST MASTERS

631.	Darren Anderton
632.	Ricky Villa
633.	Glenn Hoddle (19 goals)
634.	Mark Falco
635.	Steve Archibald
636.	Graham Roberts
637.	Clive Allen (his father was Les Allen)
638.	Jimmy Greaves (v Blackpool)
639.	Martin Chivers (8 goals)
640.	Bobby Smith

SPURS AT THE WORLD CUP - 1

641.	Darren Anderton
642.	Glenn Hoddle
643.	Ilie Dumitrescu
644.	Gary Lineker

645. Ricky Villa
646. Alf Ramsey
647. Nico Claesen
648. Richard Gough
649. Danny Blanchflower
650. Erik Thorstvedt

SOUNDS LIKE

651. Clive Allen
652. Bert Bliss
653. Anthony Gardner
654. Ledley King
655. Tim Sherwood
656. Stephen Carr
657. Alan Brazil
658. Paul Gascoigne
659. Noureddine Naybet
660. Mike England

TERRY VENABLES

661. 1987 (November)
662. Liverpool
663. Derby County (First Division away game on 20 December 1987)
664. Clive Allen & Nico Claesen
665. 137
666. 68
667. 1991
668. Manchester United (on 20 May 1991 - the FA Cup Final win over Nottingham Forest was 2 days earlier)
669. Hendry
670. Southampton (2-0)

TRIVIA - 10

671. Titanic (The Daily Telegraph Titanic Fund - Spurs lost 3-0)
672. Bill Nicholson
673. 2000-2001
674. Terry Fenwick
675. Tim Sherwood
676. 10
677. Willem Korsten
678. Terry Venables
679. Cliff Jones
680. Luton Town

CAPPED AT SPURS

681. South Africa   Mbulelo Mabizela
682. Sweden   Erik Edman
683. Switzerland   Ramon Vega
684. USA   Kasey Keller
685. Portugal   Helder Postiga
686. Yugoslavia   Goran Bunjevcevic
687. Iceland   Gudni Bergsson
688. Israel   Ronny Rosenthal

| 689. | Argentina | Ossie Ardiles |
| 690. | Algeria | Moussa Saib |

LEGEND - STEVE ARCHIBALD

691.	1980
692.	Aberdeen
693.	£800,000
694.	20
695.	Wolverhampton Wanderers
696.	6
697.	Garth Crooks
698.	1984
699.	Barcelona
700.	Airdrie

ODDS AND ENDS

701.	Boca Juniors
702.	Bayer Leverkusen
703.	Jenas & Stalteri
704.	£18.6million
705.	Jermain Defoe
706.	5th
707.	Dawson & Lennon
708.	MK Dons
709.	Dimitar Berbatov (£10,999,999 - Sergei Rebrov cost £11m)
710.	Mansion

THE MANAGEMENT GAME

711.	David Pleat
712.	Martin Jol
713.	52 (14 goals)
714.	Arthur Rowe
715.	Terry Venables, Glenn Hoddle & Ossie Ardiles
716.	Ipswich Town
717.	Swindon Town (Ossie Ardiles & Glenn Hoddle)
718.	Steve Perryman
719.	George Graham
720.	Sheffield Wednesday

LEGEND - GARTH CROOKS

721.	1980
722.	Stoke City (15 goals in 1979-1980)
723.	16
724.	£600,000
725.	The FA Cup Semi-Final Replay and FA Cup Final Replay
726.	Wolverhampton Wanderers
727.	Manchester United
728.	10
729.	6
730.	West Bromwich Albion

TERRY VENABLES - ENGLAND MANAGER

731. The game was abandoned after 27 minutes as a result of England fans rioting in one of the stands (Ireland were winning 1-0 at the time)
732. Denmark
733. The Umbro Cup
734. Brazil, Japan & Sweden
735. Elland Road, Leeds (3-3 v Sweden)
736. Gareth Southgate (12 December 1995)
737. Sol Campbell & Ian Walker
738. The 2 players were the Neville brothers and it was the first time 2 brothers had represented England in the same game since the Charlton brothers during the 1960s
739. Stefan Kuntz
740. Rene Higuita

SEASON 1999-2000

741. West Ham United
742. 15
743. Newcastle United
744. Newcastle United (3-1 at White Hart Lane)
745. Tim Sherwood
746. Coventry City
747. Fulham
748. David Ginola (in the FA Cup 3rd Round Replay 6-1 defeat - see Q743)
749. Steffen Iversen
750. Manchester United

TRIVIA - 11

751. Martin Jol (with ADO Den Haag Amateurs)
752. Neil Sullivan
753. Alan Gilzean & Alan Mullery
754. Jamie Carragher
755. Terry Gibson
756. 70
757. Steve Archibald
758. Ricky Villa (against Manchester City in 1981)
759. Gerry Armstrong
760. Colombia (England won 2-0)

FA CUP WINNERS - 1981

761. Queen's Park Rangers
762. Garth Crooks, Tony Galvin & Glenn Hoddle
763. Hull City
764. Keith Burkinshaw
765. Wolverhampton Wanderers
766. 3 (1 in the Semi-Final and 2 in the Final Replay)
767. Garth Crooks
768. 1-1 (3-2 in the Final Replay)
769. Exeter City (David Pleat)
770. 3

SPURS AT THE WORLD CUP - 2

771. Darren Anderton
772. Gica Popescu

773.	Chris Waddle
774.	Teddy Sheringham
775.	Jimmy Greaves
776.	Ray Clemence
777.	Dave Mackay
778.	Nico Claesen
779.	Robbie Keane
780.	Gary Lineker

LEGEND - GARY MABBUTT

781.	Bristol Rovers
782.	South Africa
783.	16
784.	The FA Video Panel (to review refereeing decisions)
785.	1991
786.	Diabetes (he once went into a coma after missing an insulin injection)
787.	Bobby Moore
788.	The UEFA Cup (1984)
789.	Kenny Dalglish
790.	John Fashanu (Wimbledon)

OPPONENTS - 3

791.	4 (Hull, Exeter, Coventry & Manchester City)
792.	Wimbledon (away)
793.	Charlton Athletic (4-1 away) & Everton (4-1 at home)
794.	Arsenal
795.	Newcastle United
796.	9-0 (against Keflavik in the 1st Round of the 1971-1972 UEFA Cup)
797.	Norwich City (at home)
798.	Vitesse Arnhem
799.	Leicester City (95 goals in 194 games)
800.	Newcastle United (4-1 at home)

SEASON 1998-1999

801.	Wimbledon
802.	Sheffield Wednesday
803.	Ruel Fox (on the opening day of the season)
804.	Everton (1-0 away)
805.	Manchester United
806.	Wimbledon (FA Cup, Premier League & Worthington Cup)
807.	John Scales
808.	David Ginola
809.	Newcastle United
810.	Northampton Town (Spurs won 3-1 away)

SPURS v ARSENAL - 3

811.	Clive Allen
812.	Steve Archibald (26 December 1983 & 21 April 1984)
813.	Marc Falco (2), Chris Hughton (2) & Alan Brazil
814.	Ossie Ardiles
815.	Andy Sinton
816.	Jurgen Klinsmann
817.	Nico Claesen

818.   Gary Stevens
819.   Garth Crooks
820.   Chris Armstrong & Teddy Sheringham

LEGEND - MARTIN CHIVERS
821.   1968
822.   Southampton
823.   Jimmy Greaves
824.   Sheffield Wednesday
825.   Aston Villa (in a 4-1 2nd Round League Cup win)
826.   Alan Gilzean
827.   Greece (2004 winners)
828.   17
829.   Dunfermline Athletic
830.   Servette

LEGEND - RICKY VILLA
831.   1978
832.   Buenos Aires (18 August 1952)
833.   Nottingham Forest (19 August 1978)
834.   1988
835.   Miami Strikers
836.   Deportivo Cali (Colombia)
837.   124
838.   18
839.   1981-1982
840.   The FA Cup (1981)

TRIVIA - 12
841.   52
842.   Germany, Saudi Arabia & Spain
843.   David Pleat
844.   Martin Chivers
845.   Clive Allen
846.   Ronny Rosenthal
847.   Nico Claesen
848.   £450,000
849.   England
850.   851

I PLAYED FOR SPURS & ARSENAL
851.   Rohan Ricketts (July 2002 - free transfer)
852.   Pat Jennings
853.   Willie Young
854.   Narada Bernard
855.   David Black (May 1898)
856.   Pat Jennings (from Spurs to Arsenal in 1977, from Arsenal to Spurs in 1985)
857.   £80,000 (for Willie Young from Spurs to Arsenal in March 1977)
858.   George Graham
859.   £nil (he signed for Arsenal for free on a 'Bosman Ruling')
860.   Kevin Stead & Steve Walford

SPURS v WEST HAM UNITED

861.   Jimmy Greaves (12)
862.   Mauricio Taricco (November 2004)
863.   Michael Carrick (August 2004)
864.   £7 million
865.   Bobby Zamora
866.   Gary Lineker
867.   5
868.   10-0 (9 January 1905)
869.   6-1 (25 August 1962)
870.   Clive Allen

LEAGUE CUP WINNERS - 1971

871.   Swansea City
872.   Martin Peters
873.   West Bromwich Albion
874.   Coventry City
875.   Martin Chivers
876.   Sheffield United
877.   Bristol City
878.   Aston Villa
879.   Martin Chivers
880.   Alan Gilzean

LEGEND - MARTIN PETERS

881.   West Ham United
882.   1970 (March)
883.   London (8 November 1943)
884.   Coventry City
885.   The League Cup (1971)
886.   FC Nantes
887.   24
888.   287
889.   87
890.   Norwich City

TRIVIA - 13

891.   Martin Chivers
892.   Coventry City (4-0 away)
893.   No. 4
894.   Martin Peters
895.   1
896.   Bobby Zamora
897.   Clive Allen (1986-87)
898.   £150,000 (summer 1974)
899.   1989
900.   George Graham

FA CUP WINNERS - 1982

901.   Spurs were the FA Cup holders
902.   Arsenal
903.   Garth Crooks
904.   Leicester City (Spurs beat them to win the "Double" in 1961)

905.	Queen's Park Rangers
906.	Glenn Hoddle
907.	Leeds United
908.	Chelsea
909.	Steve Archibald & Micky Hazard
910.	Aston Villa

LEGEND - GLENN HODDLE

911.	1975
912.	17
913.	1
914.	Stoke City
915.	Bolton Wanderers (3rd Round, 7 January 1978)
916.	FA Cup (1981)
917.	AS Monaco
918.	Swindon Town
919.	Chelsea
920.	1996

LONDON DERBIES

921.	Dimitar Berbatov
922.	8
923.	1 (Arsenal 2-2 at home)
924.	Charlton Athletic (4-2 away)
925.	Arsenal, Charlton Athletic, Chelsea, Fulham & West Ham United
926.	Chelsea (0-0 at home & 1-1 away)
927.	Crystal Palace (1-1 at home)
928.	Chelsea (lost 2-0 at home)
929.	Wimbledon
930.	Jurgen Klinsmann

LEGEND - ALAN MULLERY

931.	Fulham
932.	1964
933.	£72,500
934.	The FA Cup in 1967
935.	FWA Footballer of the Year Award
936.	35
937.	1970 (Mexico)
938.	Fulham
939.	The FA Cup Final (Fulham lost the 1975 FA Cup Final to West Ham United)
940.	An MBE

TRIVIA - 14

941.	Tony the Tiger in a Frosties advertisement
942.	Jurgen Klinsmann
943.	Martin Peters (he joined Norwich City)
944.	4
945.	John Motson
946.	Terry Venables
947.	25
948.	Sergei Rebrov
949.	Christian Ziege

950.   Bobby Smith (1961 & 1962)

JUANDE RAMOS
951.   Elche
952.   Alcoyano, Linares, Eldense, Alicante & Denia
953.   Midfielder
954.   Alcoyano
955.   Middlesbrough (4-0)
956.   FC Barcelona (3-0)
957.   Manchester City
958.   Blackpool (in the Carling Cup)
959.   Gustavo Poyet
960.   Birmingham City

LEAGUE CUP WINNERS - 1973
961.   Huddersfield Town
962.   Middlesbrough
963.   3
964.   Wolverhampton Wanderers
965.   Martin Peters
966.   Liverpool
967.   Millwall
968.   Norwich City
969.   Ralph Coates
970.   Martin Peters (5 goals)

FA CUP WINNERS - 1967
971.   Chelsea
972.   Tottenham Hotspur 2 Chelsea 1
973.   Nottingham Forest
974.   Millwall
975.   Terry Venables (managed Spurs to victory in 1991)
976.   Birmingham City
977.   Jimmy Greaves (6 goals)
978.   Frank Saul
979.   Bristol City
980.   Dave Mackay

LEGEND - DAVE MACKAY
981.   1959 (March)
982.   Hearts
983.   £30,000
984.   Ron Henry
985.   Derby County
986.   West Ham United
987.   Noel Cantwell
988.   Tony Book
989.   Derby County
990.   Kuwait

TRIVIA - 15
991.   Tim Sherwood (Blackburn Rovers won the Premier League in season 1994-95)

148

992.   Ray Clemence
993.   Glenn Hoddle
994.   Martin Peters
995.   He is the only Spurs player to have scored 3 hat-tricks in consecutive games
        for the club (October - November 1925)
996.   Jurgen Klinsmann
997.   676 (plus over 300 more for Arsenal)
998.   57
999.   Andy Gray
1000.   Diamond Lights

LEGEND - DAVID GINOLA
1001.   Newcastle United
1002.   1997 (15 July)
1003.   Matra Racing Paris (later renamed Racing Paris 1)
1004.   Tim Flowers (he won the Premiership with Blackburn Rovers in 1995)
1005.   Queen's Park Rangers (at Loftus Road)
1006.   Chelsea (in 1995-1996 for Newcastle United)
1007.   French Player of the Year and French Players' Player of the Year
1008.   1998-1999
1009.   Aston Villa
1010.   The Red Cross Anti-Landmine Campaign

LEGEND - TEDDY SHERINGHAM
1011.   Millwall
1012.   Nottingham Forest
1013.   1992
1014.   £2.1 million
1015.   51
1016.   1997
1017.   Spurs (10 August 1997 at White Hart Lane)
1018.   Portsmouth
1019.   The Inter-Continental Cup (World Club Championship)
1020.   West Ham United

LEGEND - ERIK THORSTVEDT
1021.   1988 (December)
1022.   Terry Venables
1023.   Kuwait (13 November 1982)
1024.   The Olympic Games in Los Angeles, USA
1025.   Borussia Munchengladbach
1026.   Bobby Mimms
1027.   Erik The Viking
1028.   Ian Walker
1029.   97
1030.   Wolverhampton Wanderers

JERMAIN DEFOE
1031.   Beckton (on 7 October 1982)
1032.   Charlton Athletic
1033.   West Ham United
1034.   2004 (January)
1035.   Sweden (as a substitute 10 March 2004)

1036.	Poland (it was his full debut)
1037.	Chelsea
1038.	18
1039.	Bournemouth
1040.	Portsmouth

LEGEND - CHRIS HUGHTON
1041.	Irish
1042.	53
1043.	An engineer
1044.	297 (293 plus 4 as a substitute)
1045.	The FA Cup in 1981
1046.	Coach (Stewart Houston was the assistant manager to George Graham)
1047.	1990
1048.	QPR (17 March 1990)
1049.	The 1984 UEFA Cup
1050.	Brian Kerr (the Republic of Ireland manager)

EXPERT:
EXPERT - BILL NICHOLSON
1051.	Northfleet
1052.	Blackburn Rovers (22 October 1938 in a Division 2 game, Spurs lost 3-1)
1053.	Darlington, Manchester United, Middlesbrough, Newcastle United, Sunderland & Fulham (1 game)
1054.	Portugal (1951)
1055.	Arthur Rowe
1056.	Danny Blanchflower & Johnny Giles
1057.	Keith Burkinshaw
1058.	West Ham United
1059.	1974 UEFA Cup Final
1060.	Club President

EXPERT - HISTORY
1061.	Harry Hotspur
1062.	Tottenham Marshes
1063.	Tottenham Hotspur Football & Athletic Club
1064.	St Albans in the London Association Cup (won 5-2)
1065.	Northumberland Park
1066.	They adopted lily-white shirts
1067.	The Southern League
1068.	The cockerel & ball motif was placed on the stand
1069.	Stamford Bridge
1070.	Bruce Castle

EXPERT - WINNERS
1071.	Southern District Charity Cup	1907
1072.	Sun International Challenge Trophy	1983
1073.	London League Premier Division	1903
1074.	Football League Division 2	1920
1075.	Football League South	1945
1076.	FA Charity Shield	1952
1077.	Dewar Shield	1934

1078.	FA Cup	1921
1079.	London Challenge Cup	1929
1080.	Western League	1904

EXPERT - LEGEND - JURGEN KLINSMANN

1081.	Stuttgart Kickers (1978)
1082.	TB Gingen (1972-74) & SC Geislingen (1974-78)
1083.	Vfb Stuttgart
1084.	5
1085.	1987
1086.	108
1087.	1987-88
1088.	1988
1089.	Monaco
1090.	3rd (1995)

EXPERT - LEGEND - STEVE PERRYMAN

1091.	2
1092.	1973
1093.	Brentford
1094.	Watford (December 1990)
1095.	Middlesbrough
1096.	Ossie Ardiles
1097.	Shimizu S-Pulse
1098.	Exeter City
1099.	The Asian Cup Winners' Cup (with Shimizu S-Pulse in 2000)
1100.	Kashiwa Reysol

EXPERT - SPURS v ARSENAL

1101.	11 (19 March 2000 - 13 November 2004)
1102.	9
1103.	Billy Minter & Bobby Smith
1104.	110
1105.	40
1106.	Terry Dyson
1107.	7
1108.	The referee stopped the game following the use of bad language by the players (Arsenal were winning 2-1 at the time and the result stood)
1109.	London Professional Football Charity Fund
1110.	The London War Cup

EXPERT - TRIMA - 1

1111.	7
1112.	The Dentist's Chair (in Hong Kong)
1113.	4
1114.	Japan (J-League Second Stage Championship in 1999)
1115.	1988
1116.	Leicester City
1117.	1995
1118.	Burnley
1119.	Gansu Tianma
1120.	Manchester City

EXPERT - SPURS v CHELSEA

1121. Glenn Hoddle
1122. Johnny Brooks (to Chelsea) & Les Allen (to Spurs)
1123. Jason Cundy
1124. £2 million (Gordon Durie to Spurs in August 1991)
1125. Mark Falco
1126. Sol Campbell
1127. Pearce, Perryman, Peters & Pratt
1128. Stephane Dalmat & Paul Konchesky
1129. Alex Wright
1130. Rory Allen

EXPERT - LEGEND - JIMMY GREAVES

1131. The European Cup Winners' Cup
1132. Nottingham Forest
1133. 35
1134. Alan Gilzean
1135. He got Hepatitis B
1136. Geoff Hurst
1137. The FA Cup
1138. 44
1139. West Ham United
1140. Martin Peters

EXPERT - CUP FINALS

1141. John Cameron
1142. Jimmy Banks, Jimmy Cantrell, Jimmy Dimmock & Jimmy Seed
1143. Bill Brown
1144. 7 (3 FA Cups, 2 League Cups, 1 ECWC & 1 UEFA Cup)
1145. Bill Nicholson (1971 & 1973), Keith Burkinshaw (1982), George Graham
(1999) & Glenn Hoddle (2002)
1146. Ossie Ardiles
1147. Spurs 4, Anderlecht 3
1148. Danny Thomas
1149. Martin Chivers
1150. Cliff Jones

EXPERT - TERRY VENABLES

1151. 28
1152. 7
1153. Paul Stewart
.1154. Luton Town
1155. Liverpool (2-1 at White Hart Lane)
1156. Nottingham Forest (League & FA Cup 1991 Final)
1157. Paul Gascoigne & Paul Stewart
1158. Denmark (3 April 1994)
1159. Germany (Euro'96 Semi-Final defeat on penalties at Wembley)
1160. Darren Anderton (England won 5-0)

EXPERT - TRIVIA - 2

1161. Colin Clarke (v Queen's Park Rangers)
1162. The Dutch Player of the Year Award
1163. Garth Crooks

1164.	Jimmy Greaves & Terry Dyson
1165.	48
1166.	Nico Claesen
1167.	Clive Allen
1168.	The Football League carried out an investigation to make sure that there was nothing illegal about the transfer (his old club, Chelsea, had also bid for him)
1169.	Jimmy Greaves
1170.	Steffen Iversen (v IFC Kaiserslautern in the 1999-2000 UEFA Cup)

EXPERT - LEGEND - GARY MABBUTT

1171.	Lyon & Atletico Madrid
1172.	8
1173.	Keith Burkinshaw
1174.	37
1175.	2
1176.	1987 (an own goal against Coventry City)
1177.	1982
1178.	£105,000 (from Bristol Rovers)
1179.	An MBE
1180.	West Germany (debut - 1982) & Yugoslavia (goal - 1986)

EXPERT - LEGEND - MARTIN CHIVERS

1181.	Southampton (27 April 1945)
1182.	£125,000
1183.	1975-1976
1184.	Sheffield United (in a 5-0 home win)
1185.	367
1186.	Bill Nicholson & Terry Neill
1187.	1972-1973
1188.	Lyn Oslo
1189.	174
1190.	Newcastle United (as a substitute in a 3-0 home defeat)

EXPERT - SPURS v WEST HAM UNITED

1191.	69,118 (3 March 1956)
1192.	43,322 (17 October 1970 - West Ham United's record attendance)
1193.	5-0 (on 16 March 1918)
1194.	5-0 (on 8 October 1906)
1195.	10 (Spurs won 10-0 on 9 January 1905)
1196.	Matthew Etherington
1197.	Les Ferdinand
1198.	Paul Allen
1199.	It was Spurs' first ever game in the League Cup
1200.	Jurgen Klinsmann

EXPERT - LEGEND - GLENN HODDLE

1201.	1991
1202.	1993
1203.	Howard Wilkinson
1204.	George Graham
1205.	Eileen Drewery
1206.	Southampton
1207.	Martin Chivers

1208.	Terry Neill
1209.	First Division Play-Offs 1993
1210.	Glenn Hoddle: My 1998 World Cup Diary Book

EXPERT - TRIVIA - 3

1211.	Martin Chivers
1212.	Manchester United (4-1 at home)
1213.	Ricky Villa
1214.	Martin Peters
1215.	49 (33 League & 16 Cup)
1216.	West Ham United (on 29 October 1994)
1217.	39
1218.	7
1219.	47
1220.	Steve Archibald

EXPERT - LEGEND - JOHN PRATT

1221.	1965 (November)
1222.	Arsenal
1223.	The Portland Timbers
1224.	Peter Shreeves
1225.	Danny Blanchflower
1226.	415
1227.	49
1228.	Stoke City
1229.	The UEFA Cup in 1972
1230.	Gordon Banks (Stoke City) & Ray Clemence (Liverpool)

EXPERT - LEGEND - JOHN WHITE

1231.	Falkirk
1232.	He was a soldier in the Army on National Service
1233.	He was a champion cross-country runner
1234.	£22,000
1235.	1959
1236.	The Ghost
1237.	The League Championship in 1961
1238.	183
1239.	47
1240.	He was struck by lightning whilst taking shelter under a tree during a round of golf (Crews Hill Golf Course)

EXPERT - LEGEND - DARREN ANDERTON

1241.	1992
1242.	Portsmouth
1243.	£1,750,000
1244.	30
1245.	7
1246.	Southampton (7 February 1993 at White Hart Lane)
1247.	Sicknote
1248.	The League Cup (v Brentford on 7 October 1992 away)
1249.	358
1250.	48